SOFTWARE TESTING

THE McGRAW-HILL INTERNATIONAL
SOFTWARE QUALITY ASSURANCE SERIES

Consulting Editor

Professor D. Ince
The Open University

Other titles in this series

Practical Implementation of Software Metrics	Goodman
Software Testing	Roper
Software Metrics for Product Assessment	Bache and Bazzana

Related titles on software engineering are published in an accompanying series: **The International Software Engineering Series**, also edited by Professor Darrel Ince.

SOFTWARE TESTING

Marc Roper
Strathclyde University

McGRAW-HILL BOOK COMPANY

London · New York · St Louis · San Francisco · Auckland · Bogotá · Caracas
Lisbon · Madrid · Mexico · Milan · Montreal · New Delhi · Panama
Paris · San Juan · São Paulo · Singapore · Sydney · Tokyo · Toronto

Published by
McGRAW-HILL Book Company Europe
SHOPPENHANGERS ROAD · MAIDENHEAD · BERKSHIRE · SL6 2QL · ENGLAND
TELEPHONE 0628 23432
FAX 0628 770224

British Library Cataloguing in Publication Data

Roper, Marc
   Software Testing. –
   (International Software Quality Assurance Series)
   I. Title II. Series
   005.30287

   ISBN 0–07–707466–1

Library of Congress Cataloging-in-Publication Data

Roper, Marc,
   Software testing / Marc Roper.
     p.   cm.
   Includes bibliographical references and index.
   ISBN 0–07–707466–1 :
   1. Computer software—Testing.
   I. Title.
   QA76.76.T48R65   1994
   005.1'4–dc20   93–9059
                           CIP

1234 CUP 9654

Typeset by TecSet Ltd
and printed and bound in Great Britain at the University Press, Cambridge

CONTENTS

PREFACE

Software testing has never had the grand appeal that adorns some areas of computer science. No one could accuse it of being (or ever having been) a 'fashionable' area of study. Nevertheless, over the years, many highly talented people have been attracted to the area and have contributed to its development. Why? The mundane answer is because it is there. We develop software and we have to test it—so let us find out a little more about how we do this. However, there are other reasons that attract people to do research in the area—it is a big, difficult problem that is not going to go away. It is well known that we cannot show programs to be correct by testing them. So the goal, when developing testing methods, is to be able to take any program and produce the smallest amount of test data that will give you the greatest amount of information about that program. It is challenges like this, and probably many other reasons, that attract people to carry out research in the field.

The aim of this book is to pull together the majority of work that has been carried out in the area of software testing. It has been written with a number of people in mind: the practitioner who wants to apply state-of-the-art techniques to the production of software, the researcher in software engineering who wants a detailed overview of the subject, and the advanced undergraduate or postgraduate student who is studying the subject either in its own right or as part of a software engineering course.

The book is organized in the following way. Chapter 1 gives an overview of the subject of software testing and the problems associated with it. Chapter 2 is a detailed study of errors, faults and failures. Chapter 3 contains descriptions and detailed applications of around 20 different testing techniques. Chapter 4 looks at the way in which the testing techniques may be applied to the different products of the software engineering life-cycle and considers the work that has been carried out in developing techniques to test programs written in different language paradigms. Chapter 5 is a case study that examines some of the ideas introduced in Chapter 4 in more detail.

This book has taken a long time to write (mainly due to the ever-increasing demands on the time available to carry out such research) and I would like to acknowledge the tolerance shown and encouragement given by my wife and ever-increasing number of children, the assistance given by colleagues and reviewers—especially Darrel Ince—in providing useful comments on this book, and the faith and patience exhibited by Jacqueline Harbor and others at McGraw-Hill.

QUALITY ASSURANCE FORUM

The Quality Assurance Forum is pleased to publish jointly with McGraw-Hill this book which covers topics pertinent to software quality assurance.

The aim of the organization is 'to help the member organizations improve the quality of their computer services through the exchange of information between members and with other organizations with similar interests'.

The QA Forum has over 200 members, including organizations from all sectors of industry and commerce, as well as local and national government. While these organizations are predominantly based in the UK, this includes a growing number from other countries in Europe.

This series of books aims to provide an opportunity for authors to publish works which are both practical and state-of-the-art. In this way QA Forum members and other organizations will benefit from the exchange of information and the development of new ideas which will further the cause of quality in Information Technology.

The QA Forum publishes these books with the aim of stimulating discussion in the software community so that the industry as a whole will move forward to improved products and services. It is proud to be associated with the series while not endorsing every single point of view in every book.

If you would like to know more about the QA Forum, please contact:

Quality Assurance Forum
17 St Catherine's Rd
Ruislip
Middlesex HA4 7RX
UK
Tel: +44 (0) 895 635222
Fax: +44 (0) 895 679178

For Catherine, Caitlin, Madeleine and Lily

1

INTRODUCTION

1.1 WHAT IS SOFTWARE TESTING?

Although as old as the first program, software testing only came to be treated as a serious research topic in the late sixties when the 'software crisis' spawned the concept of software engineering. To clarify matters from the start, it is appropriate to consider the various definitions that have been given to software testing. Adrion, *et al*. (1982) define it as:

> Examination of the behaviour of a program by executing the program on sample data sets,

while Glass (1979) defines it as:

> . . . the process of executing computer software in order to determine whether the results it produces are correct.

Myers (1979) is of the opinion that testing adds some 'value metric' to the program in that the discovery and removal of errors increases the reliability and quality of the program. His definition of testing is:

> . . . the process of executing a program with the intent of finding errors.

This almost aggressive approach to the subject can be seen as a response to Dijkstra's, (Dahl *et al*. (1972)) comment some years earlier that,

> Program testing can be used to show the presence of bugs, but never their absence.

This, however, is not true. As will be seen later, there are testing methods that are able to show certain—but not *all*—'bugs' (or faults) to be absent. A contrast to Myers' approach is made by Hennell *et al.* (1984) who argue that:

> the aim . . . is not to discover errors but to provide convincing evidence that there are none

or,

> . . . to show that particular classes [of fault] are not present.

Hetzel devotes a large section of *The Complete Guide to Software Testing* (1985) to the definition of testing and concludes:

> Testing is any activity aimed at evaluating an attribute or capability of a program or system. Testing is the measurement of software quality.

In the above definitions there is a tendency to refer to *program* testing. It should be noted that there is no intention in this book to restrict the discussion to program testing and ignore the issues associated with testing different aspects of software, such as systems. Admittedly most research has been carried out on programs and most of the testing techniques were developed for programs (and programs are often used to demonstrate their usage), but this does not preclude their application to different software objects. Indeed, in the definitions, one can substitute the word 'program' with any appropriate alternative such as 'system' or 'subsystem' without loss of meaning—as we shall see later.

Readers should not let themselves be confused or discouraged by this number of definitions. I feel it is largely due to a combination of the passion and enthusiasm that people feel for the subject and the youthful nature of the field of software engineering in which there are relatively few rigid definitions. Essentially there are very few differences between the definitions, and what differences exist are largely matters of belief or attitude. They can be classified into those that are a straightforward description of the process, those that advocate an aggressive 'bug-hunting' approach, and those that consider the consequences in terms of the 'quality' of the software under test. I would suggest that the reader chooses whichever definition he or she finds most useful and appropriate. As an alternative, there is the very straightforward definition put forward by a prominent British researcher in testing:

> Testing is just sampling.

1.2 WHY TEST SOFTWARE?

In manufacturing industries, testing plays a very distinct role. In producing anything from complex electronic components to plastic toys the purpose of testing is to detect duds—those products that are defective in some way. The testing may often be quite simplistic, sometimes as straightforward as a visual inspection, but more usually it will be a basic set of checks which determines whether or not the product is sold or discarded. The testing of such products is comparatively simple for two reasons: firstly, the product is well understood, secondly, the processes and materials used in its construction are also well understood and are (hopefully) being constantly monitored and possibly improved.

Software differs from such manufactured products in precisely the ways that make the testing of such products straightforward. Firstly, the product is not well understood. As Henderson (1985) states:

> There is a property of software which makes computer programming unique among the engineering disciplines. The material from which the artifacts [sic] (programs) are constructed is of a mathematical kind. The material is not found in nature and governed by physical laws, but is an artificial creation which obeys laws which we ourselves control.

Henderson goes on to argue that this potential for control has not been exploited as best it might and programming languages are so complex (in mathematical terms) that '. . . we are unable to make precise statements of the laws which the languages obey'.

Secondly, the processes are not well understood. It has been suggested that it is the processes that go into constructing software and not the software product that should be tested. If the processes are well formulated then surely the resulting product will be? Consider the processes that go into constructing a piece of software. The progression through the typical software development life-cycle, from analysis, to specification, design and on to implementation, is not a purely transformational process. Certainly, some parts of the software may be constructed by verified derivation, but the majority involves some human input, some notion of creativity or intuition. Given the differing talents and abilities possessed by individual people and the variety of environmental and personal factors that might affect their work (state of health, state of mind, training given by employer, experience, available tools and so on) it is easy to see why the processes involved in creating software cannot be readily formalized, analysed and understood.

Comparisons are often made between software engineering and other forms of engineering. 'Why can't we build software in the same way that we build bridges?' is a frequently asked, often rhetorical, question. While such comparisons are not exactly odious, they can lead to some dangerously simplistic assumptions. Bridge building is in some respects a valid comparison since bridges are not mass-produced and each construction project is different as regards features like the span, geology, volume and type of traffic, and weather conditions. Nevertheless, the functionality of a bridge is limited. As Ince (1988) points out 'A bridge has one main function: to carry traffic across an obstacle, subject to values of peak and average wind speed, vehicle loading, and vehicle throughput.' Compare this with the typical functionality of a piece of software—for example, an operating system, spreadsheet or video game. Having said that the functionality of a bridge is limited is not to imply that bridge building is easy or that engineers do not occasionally get it wrong. Spectacular failures like the Tacoma Narrows have prompted engineers to analyse what went wrong and to modify their theories and practices in the light of these mistakes. It must of course be remembered that software construction is a very new discipline and cannot be expected to have the maturity of engineering practices such as bridge building. I do not wish to pursue this analogy any further. The interested reader might care to look at the work of Mary Shaw at Carnegie-Mellon University—see Shaw (1990), for example.

So why do we need to test software? We need to test it because it is not a mass-produced item, fulfilling some well-defined task. It is an individually crafted entity produced to fulfil some often very complex purpose. On top of this is the wealth of empirical evidence which reminds us that we need to be concerned about testing. Consider the amount of time that is spent upon testing. Deutsch (1982) gives figures ranging from 44 to 50 per cent for the amount of person-effort devoted to testing in the development of four space-borne projects. Boehm (1978) estimates the amount of testing (and integration) effort involved in the completion of a project to range from 28 per cent (with 28 per cent devoted to code and auditing and 44 per cent to analysis and design) for a 'business-type' project, to 50 per cent (17 per cent code and 33 per cent analysis) for operating systems, with a variety of other types of systems (spaceborne, scientific and command and control) falling within this range.

Given that a significant amount of time (and money) of a typical software project is invested in testing, it might be tempting to expect the developed software to be flawless. This is not the case. Lientz and Swanson (1980) conducted an extensive study of software maintenance and discovered that 12.4 per cent of a person's time was spent on 'program fixes' and 9.3 per cent on 'routine debugging'. It is apparent from this that at least 21.7 per cent of the maintenance activity is a direct consequence of poor testing. Having accepted that the product is not flawless, the next temptation is to think that the flaws are minor in nature. This is not the case either. Certainly some of the shortcomings of the software will be trivial, but the very nature of software, and of the objects that it is now used to control, means that even the smallest faults can have the most catastrophic consequences. As computers are introduced more and more into everyday life, the consequences of inadequate testing become even more widespread and hazardous. The computer press abounds with 'horror' stories of computer failure (due to hardware or software malfunctioning) involving a huge range of applications ranging from aircraft, medical systems, factory control systems and space-systems, all the way down to the bill for £0.00. The reasons that such faults could slip through the testing net will be considered in the next section.

1.3 PROBLEMS OF TESTING

There are obvious practical difficulties associated with testing software systems, such as having poorly expressed requirements, informal design techniques and nothing executable available until the coding stage. On top of these are the various psychological and managerial problems. Firstly, it is necessary to understand some of the fundamental difficulties of testing which are best expressed with reference to program testing but which apply at other stages of the development life-cycle.

The basic reason that the kinds of disasters described in the previous section (along with a multitude of less spectacular failures) is that testing cannot cope with the problem that it finds itself facing. For example, consider a very simple program that categorizes one exam result (in the range 0–100) into some grade. Then to *exhaustively* test that program it is necessary to test it on every element in its input domain—that is, every number between 0 and 100. This gives us 101 tests. Now, if this program was extended to deal, in some way, with two exam marks then the input domain has grown. It has become two-dimensional. To exhaustively test the program now it is necessary to select every point in the domain. This does not just mean that the two marks have to take on the values 0 to 100, it means that *every* combination of the two marks has to be tested. That is (0,0), (1,0), (2,0) . . . (99,100), (100,100). This now gives us $101 \times 101 = 10\,201$ test cases. Once we start to consider the input domains for a program which processes a record that has, say, a one-character field, two 10-byte strings and three 16-bit integers, then the number of test cases becomes enormous and the time taken to create the test data, run the tests, and check the output has to be expressed in billions of years! Testing can be thought of as choosing a subset of this input domain. The size of this subset is determined by the time available to do the testing, and its contents by the techniques employed. Obviously this subset is chosen so as to give the greatest confidence in the program under test. However, there is always the underlying fact that a set of data not included in the subset might cause the program to fail (and will inevitably be chosen by the first person to use the program after release!).

The problem of exhaustive testing is classified as being *intractable*. This means that solution using a computer (or by any other means in this case) is impossible because of the inordinate demand for resources (time).

Even if the input domain was small enough to realistically attempt exhaustive testing, another problem rears its head. There may be test cases for which the program does not halt (that is, terminate within a reasonable amount of time). It is therefore necessary to identify these cases so as to be able to complete the testing. The problem of identifying non-halting cases is classified as being *undecidable* (that is, no algorithm exists for its solution).

So far, only the domain, or input space of a program has been taken into account. It is also important to consider the internal structure of a program under test. This is best described with some very simple examples (in this case, reading a number, finding its square root, and outputting the result). The language used for the examples is a simple pseudocode—the syntax and semantics of which are unimportant since it is the basic structure of the program, or algorithm, that must be emphasized. To do this, the *directed graph* representation is shown beside the programs. A directed graph consists of nodes connected by arcs (or edges) with arrows to indicate direction. The nodes represent blocks of statements (a block of code is defined such that if the first statement is executed then so are all subsequent statements) and the edges indicate precedence (or transfer of control)—see, for example, Marimont (1960) or Lipow (1975) for more information on the subject. This allows the structure of the program to be examined independently of the function. In the examples below, the blocks have been numbered for ease of reference.

Figure 1.1 shows the simple case where there is just one path (that is, a route from the start of the program to the end) through the program. Suppose it is necessary to filter out any negative numbers to avoid dealing with complex numbers as shown in Fig. 1.2. There are now two paths through the program. One, *ac*, is where the number is greater than zero and the square root is found and printed. The other, *bd*, is where the number is less than or equal to zero and an error message is printed. Extending the program further, a loop is introduced so that it does not have to be repeatedly executed to process another number. This extension is shown in Fig. 1.3. The program will continue to process numbers until presented with a zero. The situation has now become a lot more complex following the introduction of a loop.

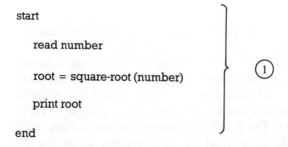

Figure 1.1 Program with one path.

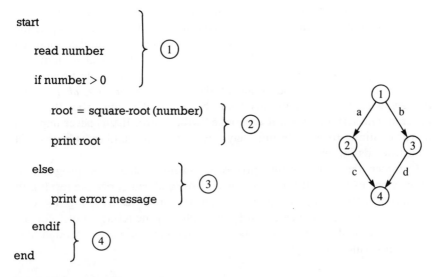

Figure 1.2 Program with two paths.

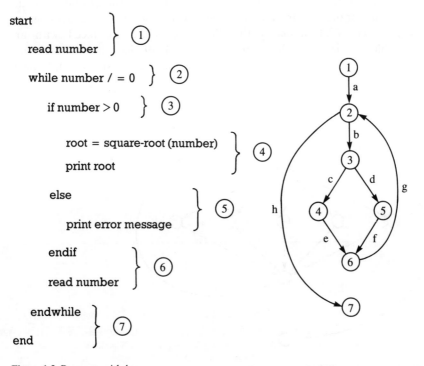

Figure 1.3 Program with loop.

The strict definition of a path through a program means that the number of loop repetitions must be taken into account. For example, the path followed by executing the program on one positive number followed by a zero is different from the path taken by two positive numbers followed by a zero, even though the route taken through the program is identical in both cases. So, some of the paths are: *abcegh, abcegbcegh, abcegbcegbcegh*, ... This raises another issue. The only way that this program will terminate is if it is supplied with a zero. If this never happens it will continue to execute infinitely and hence the number of paths will tend towards infinity.

Consider the exam results processing example again. A program to process one exam result for up to ten students and categorize the result into the classes I, II(i), II(ii), III and Fail could be represented as in Fig. 1.4. One branch is required for each category of result and the return branch for the loop is executed up to nine times. The number of paths through this program is calculated by:

$$\sum_{i=1}^{n+1} x^i$$

where n is the maximum number of loop iterations (nine) and x is the number of branches or decisions within the loop (five). This gives approximately *12.4 million* paths! Once again we are faced with an intractable problem. Furthermore, Weyuker (1979) has shown that there is no algorithm that can determine whether or not a given statement, branch

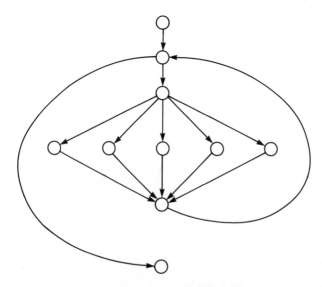

Figure 1.4 Directed graph of exam results program.

or path in a program may be exercised, or whether or not every such unit may be exercised. So, even if the number of paths through a program was a reasonable number, it would be undecidable to determine which, or if all, of them would be executable.

Knowing that the discipline of software testing is inhabited by undecidable and intractable problems is what makes it such an interesting and challenging area to work in!

1.4 THE ROLE OF TESTING IN SOFTWARE ENGINEERING

This section gives some background to the subject of testing. It introduces terminology and topics that will be covered in more detail later in the book and talks a little about the process of testing software.

1.4.1 Some background

Historically there have emerged different classifications of testing techniques. Although these will be covered in more detail later in the book, it is worthwhile introducing much of the terminology at this point.

Some earlier review papers make a distinction between *static* and *dynamic* testing techniques. Static techniques were those that examined the software without executing it and encompassed activities such as inspection, symbolic execution, and verification. Dynamic techniques are those that examined the software with a view to generating test data for execution by the software. In this book it is solely the dynamic techniques with which we are concerned.

Another set of terms that needs immediate explanation is the *black-box/white-box* dichotomy. Test cases that were derived without reference to the construction of the program (i.e. they were created by reference to the specification, or some other description of what the software should do) were termed 'black-box' techniques. That is, the software was treated as a black box and its functionality was determined by supplying it with different combinations of inputs. In contrast to this, test cases that were derived by examination of the construction of the program (its 'internal workings') were then termed 'white-box'. Other terms have been introduced over the years and now black-box techniques are sometimes called 'functional' or 'specification-based' and white-box techniques may be referred to as 'structural' or 'code-based' or even 'glass-box'.

It is important to examine why this distinction appeared. Black-box techniques are frequently a vague formalization of good testing practice. Their drawback is that without examining the code in some way you do not know how much of it is being tested. Black-box techniques are typically used to check if the product conforms to its specification. But what if there is something in the product that does not meet the specification? What if the software performs some undesirable task that the black-box inputs have not detected? This is where white-box techniques come in. They allow you to examine the code in detail and be confident that at least you have achieved a level of test coverage such as execution of every statement. White-box techniques are in themselves insufficient since the software under examination may not perform one of its desired tasks—the function to do this may even be missing—and examination of the code is unlikely to reveal this. The objective perspective of black-box testing is needed to be able to spot such missing functionality. This relationship between black-box and white-box testing is shown in Fig. 1.5.

The early testing techniques were preoccupied with achieving and defining higher levels of coverage (i.e. testing the program more thoroughly) based on the structure of the program (e.g. statement, branch and multiple condition coverage, LCSAJs, etc.) or the way it used data (data flow testing). The last ten years or so have seen a growing interest in the techniques of fault-based testing (weak and strong mutation) which, instead of trying to exercise the program with more and more data, have concentrated on trying to generate data that revealed likely faults in the program. It was almost as if testing had spied its quarry—faults—and was out to get them! With the collection of accurate and reliable fault-data, it is this kind of technique that could become very powerful in the future.

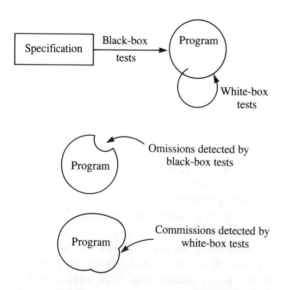

Figure 1.5 Relationship between black-box and white-box testing techniques.

1.4.2 The testing process

The testing process is shown diagrammatically in Fig. 1.6. The testing process is one that takes its input from some product of the software process and whose output is applied either to the product from which the tests were derived or to some other subsequent product. Preferably, this application is in the form of execution, although use of test data for such activities as walkthroughs and reviews is encouraged. Finally, the results of the application are checked against an 'oracle'. An oracle is something that can decide unequivocally whether or not the output produced from the tests is correct. In practice, an oracle would be a specification, a design document, or a set of requirements, for example.

In applying testing to the life-cycle, a bottom-up approach is employed. The lowest-level modules, procedures or functions are usually the first executable items to be produced. These should be tested by their producers using the *structural* or *white-box* and *functional* or *black-box* techniques. At this point, the subject under test is relatively small and so can be subjected to a high degree of testing.

The next step is to test the groupings of functions and procedures into modules (defined by one specification), and this should be done by an independent party (i.e. *not* the programmer) deriving tests from the specification.

Following this comes the integration testing stage, in which all the modules are linked together. Finally there is the systems testing stage in which the testing concentrates on checking whether the system does what is required.

The procedure is one that starts at the microscopic level and gradually 'moves up' to incorporate items of larger complexity and test them at a higher level of abstraction.

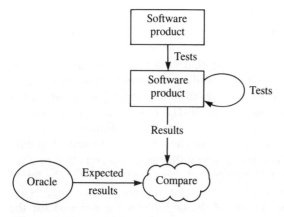

Figure 1.6 Diagram of the testing process.

Perhaps the hardest part of the testing process to tackle is the psychological aspect. Testing can be seen as a highly destructive activity, designed to break our latest, lovingly created program. It is rather like a potter being asked to demonstrate the strength of his or her pots by dropping them on the floor. It is in these respects that the strategy outlined above can help in two ways: firstly, the use of methods and techniques by programmers means that they can be more objective about their testing and not shy away from sections of the code about which they feel uncomfortable. Secondly, the use of an independent team to carry out the black-box or functional testing means that again objectivity is improved, and the chances of the team misinterpreting the specification in the same way as the developer might have are reduced.

1.5 TESTING THEORY

Consider the use of theory in other scientific disciplines. (An interesting discussion on this topic is to be found in Turski and Maibaum (1987), in the section entitled 'How specifications arise'). A theory may be offered as an explanation and may subsequently be proved or disproved, or it may be a system of rules and principles (as in, for example, probability theory). The point is that the theory is employed in some way—be it explanation, calculation or evaluation. Weyuker and Ostrand (1980) capture the essence of testing theory by suggesting:

> The primary goals of a theory of testing are to provide a basis for practical program testing methodologies, and to establish ways of determining the effectiveness of tests in detecting errors.

That is, it should be used for the development and evaluation of practical methods.

The first substantial theoretical treatment of testing appeared in a paper by Goodenough and Gerhart (1975) in an attempt to 'define the characteristics of an ideal test in a way that gives insight into the problems of testing'. Firstly, it is necessary to introduce the terminology employed. A program F has domain D. $F(d)$ is the result of executing F with some input data $d \in D$. The output specification is $\text{OUT}(d, F(d))$ and is abbreviated to $\text{OK}(d)$. A test data selection criterion C defines the conditions that the test data must meet. $\text{COMPLETE}(T, C)$ defines how C is used to select test data T. The criterion C is very demanding in that the successful execution of T (as defined in $\text{COMPLETE}(T, C)$) implies that there are *no* errors in the tested program. In order to do this C must be *reliable* and *valid*. These concepts are defined below. Verbal descriptions of the definitions are included for the reader who is easily frightened by mathematical notation!

The basis of the theory is:

1. SUCCESSFUL$(T) = (\forall t \in T)$ OK(t)

    This says that for an entire test set to be successful, all test data within the test set must produce the results as defined by the specification.

2. RELIABLE$(C) = (\forall T_1, T_2 \subseteq D)($COMPLETE$(T_1, C) \wedge$ COMPLETE $(T_2, C) \Rightarrow ($SUCCESSFUL$(T_1) \equiv$ SUCCESSFUL$(T_2)))$

    The test selection criterion C is reliable if it consistently produces test sets which are successful or consistently produces test sets which are not successful. A criterion that produced two test sets, one of which executed successfully, the other of which executed unsuccessfully, would not be considered reliable.

3. VALID$(C) = (\forall d \in D)(\neg$OK$(d) \Rightarrow (\exists T \subseteq D)($COMPLETE$(T,C) \wedge$ $\neg$SUCCESSFUL$(T)))$

    A test selection criterion C is valid if, should the program execute unsuccessfully on some datum, then it is capable of producing test data that will execute unsuccessfully. This defines its ability to reveal a fault in the program.

These definitions are combined to give Goodenough and Gerhart's fundamental theorem of testing:

$$(\exists T \subseteq D)(\exists C)(\text{COMPLETE}(T, C) \wedge \text{RELIABLE}(C) \wedge \text{VALID}(C) \wedge$$
$$\text{SUCCESSFUL(T)}) \Rightarrow (\forall d \in D)(\text{OK}(d))$$

That is, if a set of test data is chosen using a criterion that is reliable and valid, the successful execution of that test data implies that the program will produce correct results over its entire input domain.

A moment's thought will reveal that the fundamental theorem described above is equivalent to a proof of correctness of the program. What is this— just by successfully executing a program with some test data defined according to some criterion guarantees that the program is *error-free*?! The disappointment comes with the realization that it is just as hard to achieve as a formal proof of correctness.

The reasoning behind this, along with a very succinct description of Goodenough and Gerhart's theory, is to be found in a paper by Weyuker and Ostrand (1980). What they showed was that the properties, reliable and valid, essentially depend on the nature of the faults in the program (information that is obviously unavailable). Their argument was that, given an input domain and an element d belonging to that domain, there is a program which processes every element other than d correctly, but which processes d incorrectly (by simply selecting out d with an *if*-statement, for example). For this reason, the only criterion that can be guaranteed to be reliable and valid is one that selects the entire input domain as one test— that is, it exhaustively tests the program. Further difficulties are that the criterion is only reliable and valid with respect to a single program (because of the dependence on knowing which faults are present). A further consequence of this is that the properties are also not preserved through debugging—a criterion may switch to any combination of reliable and valid as faults are corrected in a program. Nor are the properties independent— every criterion is either reliable or valid. Weyuker and Ostrand demonstrate this with some very succinct examples.

They modified Goodenough and Gerhart's definitions to produce *uniformly valid* and *uniformly reliable* test criteria. This was done to remove the dependence of the criteria on the program and place it on the output specification. In this way a criterion would be reliable and valid for any program written to satisfy the specification. This was done by including the program under consideration, F, as a parameter in the definitions. However, since there is always a program that can 'beat' the tests (i.e. one that is correct on all elements in the domain except one), the only criteria that is uniformly reliable and uniformly valid is one that selects the entire input domain as a test. Once again the only answer was exhaustive testing. Following this they aimed at a slightly easier target, that of 'exposing the presence of certain specified errors or demonstrating that these errors do not occur'. This led to the approach known as *revealing subdomains* which is described further in Chapter 3.

Although Goodenough and Gerhart's paper may be regarded as seminal, especially in its presentation of a formal framework for understanding the problems associated with testing, their theory was disappointing regarding the extent to which it could be used. For example, it did not readily provide a means by which testing methods could be evaluated, compared or developed (for the reason that the only testing method which could satisfy the criteria was the exhaustive case). An attempt to do just this was made by Gourlay (1984), who advanced a formal treatment of testing and suggested ways in which it may be used to compare the relative strengths of testing methods. The idea of one testing method being stronger than another was very simplistic. A test method, M, could be considered to be at least as good as another, N, if when N found an error (for 'error' read 'fault'), then so did M. This did not allow for methods catching more frequently occurring or more serious faults (if we could define such things!). It should be noted that two methods did not have to generate the same data. Gourlay introduced the notion of a reliable method as being one that revealed a fault, should one be present (this was more in line with Goodenough and Gerhart's definition of validity). The successful execution of tests generated by a reliable method implied proof of correctness of the program under test. If a test method was stronger then it was reliable for at least the same programs and specifications. Gourlay suggested that the power of a method was the size of the sets (of programs shown correct against specifications) in its reliability relation.

Howden (1976) also used the concept of reliability in his initial discussions on the *path analysis testing strategy* and attributed it to Goodenough and Gerhart. Howden introduced the idea of a test strategy being *almost reliable*, whereby the probability of an error not being discovered is very small if the elements from the input domain are chosen at random. The input domain is viewed as an Euclidean *n*-space and the volume of the input domain subset which would not reveal an error is measured against the total input domain so as to justify the choice of *almost reliable*.

DeMillo *et al.* (1987) provide a brief introduction to the theory of testing and introduce the concept of *adequate* test data. A set of test data is considered adequate if a program behaves correctly on the test data but all incorrect programs behave incorrectly. This provides a basis for the technique of *mutation testing*.

Further excursions into the realms of testing theory were made by Cherniavsky and Statman (1988). They defined a testable class of sets as one for which a function exists which generates test data that will distinguish a set from all others. From this, testing could be considered in terms of game theory (based on the idea of distinguishing data). Using this game-theoretic approach they suggested a minimum size of test for a class of sets, and a method is poor if it does not generate this minimum test set size. However, finding this minimal size is not a trivial task.

While testing theory has made a contribution to testing research by exposing fundamental problems, it has not reached a stage whereby it may be used in the way suggested by Weyuker and Ostrand, as quoted at the beginning of this section. Perhaps the most disappointing aspect about testing theory is the (almost) constant dependency on a program (or part of it) being correct. The difficulties of proving correctness are well known and for any reasonable program it is an unreasonable proposition, to say the least. A theory that assists in the development, assessment and evaluation of testing methods will be an invaluable asset to all involved in the testing community.

2

ERRORS, FAULTS AND FAILURES

We have seen some of the consequences of inadequate software testing in Chapter 1. In this chapter we are going to take a closer look at the entities that cause so much trouble. First, the terminology used will be examined followed by a look at the subject of counting and classifying errors, faults and failures. A number of detailed empirical studies have been carried out and some of these are looked at in order to gain some insight into the general pattern of errors, faults and failures. Following this, some suggestions are made on the subject of data collection.

2.1 TERMINOLOGY

I intend to mention the word 'bug' only once in this chapter. Now that I have, I shall try not to do it again—except by way of explanation within this paragraph. The origins of the word lie in the early days of computing and relate to the story of some unfortunate insect which straddled two live wires within the computer and simultaneously committed suicide and caused the machine to malfunction. While this tale is probably apocryphal, it does convey a great deal about the meaning of the word. By using the word 'bug', the suggestion is that the thing crawled there all by itself. No one is to blame for its presence. Nobody put it there. It just ambled in. Obviously, 'bugs' do not just creep into software. Somebody *is* responsible for their presence.

Now, I am not advocating witch-hunts for the perpetrators of these misdemeanours, rather a use of terminology which acknowledges that writing software is a difficult task and that people make mistakes. For our purposes, the most appropriate terminology is that favoured by the IEEE. When developing software, people make *errors*, these become *faults* in the software which then manifest themselves as *failures* when the software is run. A failure is an observed departure from the specified behaviour of the system and is not always as catastrophic as the name implies.

Some examples might serve to explain these definitions. A very simple case might involve a program to convert a person's height in feet and inches into metres and centimetres. The program involves some checks for invalid data, one of which is specified as, 'the value of height must be in the range 2 foot to 7 foot'. The programmer duly encodes this as:

```
    .
    .
if height > 2 and height < 7 then
    .
  ( process valid data )
    .
else
    .
  ( reject as out of range )
    .
```

and introduces two faults into the code. The faults are in the range check that should have read:

```
    .
    .
if height >= 2 and height <= 7 then
    .
    .
```

The values 2 and 7 were excluded from the valid data. Some speculation could be made about the error that caused this fault—perhaps the programmer misunderstood what was written in the specification, or was unsure about it but did not bother to check with the specifier, or made a typing mistake. A failure will occur when someone tries to use the program to convert, for example, the height of a seven-foot giant into metres and centimetres. The specified behaviour is for the program to carry out the conversion. The actual behaviour is to reject the height as being out of range.

Of course, not all examples are as simple as this (but are frequently just as easy to make). There may be a requirement for a system to be portable to several machines (which has implications for the choice of language, removal of operating system dependencies, etc.), and an error was made somewhere in the process of eliciting, writing or interpreting the requirements such that the portability issue did not make its way through to the system design. This situation is going to have massive implications for the entire system if it is not spotted until the implementation stage. At best, several modules will have to be changed. At worst, the entire system will have to be rewritten into a portable language.

There are some general points to be made about the relationships between errors, faults and failures.

- People make errors. Why they do this, or what form they take, is well outside the scope of this book (and well into the realm of psychology). As was seen in the first example, many possible errors could have led to the same fault. It is simply too complex to try to consider every conceivable error.
- One error may lead to many faults. The first example above is actually a simple illustration of this. A simple misunderstanding at an early stage (for example, assuming a system is going to be processing metric rather than imperial units, or that the date is going to be in UK rather than US format) can lead to the introduction of many faults scattered throughout the implemented system. Some of the faults might be similar and some might be quite distinct. It will depend upon the nature of the error and the context of the erroneously understood data or function. As a general rule, the earlier the misunderstanding is made, the larger the number of faults will be.
- A failure may occur a 'long way' from the original fault. This is saying that there is not a simple relationship between a fault and a failure, and that a fault does not always cause an instantaneous failure. Consider the module structure chart shown in Fig. 2.1. The module labelled J might contain a fault that leads to the incorrect calculation of parameter x which is passed as a parameter through several modules (K, F, B, A, and D). Eventually x is passed to module H where it is used and causes a failure to occur. Investigation of the module in which the failure was

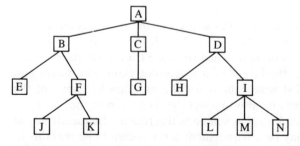

Figure 2.1 Module structure chart showing the progress of a fault through the system.

observed will, of course, not reveal the fault. This is a very simple example, and obviously the scope for propagation of incorrect values throughout a system is enormous.

- One fault may lead to many failures. Considering the previous example and referring to Fig. 2.1 again, the (incorrectly calculated) parameter x is used within module I to calculate, quite separately, values for the parameters a, b and and c which are passed to the modules L, M and N respectively. Failures then occur within modules L, M and N.

To summarize:

One error may lead to several different faults, each of which in turn leads to several different failures.

2.2 COUNTING ERRORS, FAULTS AND FAILURES

2.2.1 Perceptions of faults

Since testing is all about finding faults, it would seem natural to assume that there exists a large number of studies showing how many faults were found in a system, where they were found, by what methods and so on. These kinds of studies could tell us what kinds of faults were prevalent under particular circumstances and what testing approaches were effective. Armed with this information, the tester would then be able to approach the task of testing a system with at least some idea of where to concentrate particular resources.

Sadly, this is not the case. Since the advent of 'software engineering' about one paper per year appears dealing with this topic. Of those 20 or so papers, only a handful provide the kind of information that is genuinely useful. A possible explanation of this is that industrial companies are sensitive about releasing data that contain details about how many faults were found in a piece of software and how many errors were made in various development stages. When potential customers read this they might say, 'About product Y we are considering buying. There's a report here which says they found over 2000 faults before it was released! What a bunch of imbeciles they must be to write such fault-ridden code. Let's go and buy product Z instead'. However, the enlightened customer should realize that this means there are 2000 fewer faults for them to worry about when they start using the product. What is needed is a change of culture whereby companies do not hide this kind of information but make it openly available as a testament to the effectiveness of their testing procedures.

If this state of unabashed openness is achieved in the future then another problem will arise. If companies publish fault figures for products, how does the customer then choose between two products, one that had 1000 faults in development and the other that had 1500? Should the customer be impressed solely by the testing (and choose the product with the higher fault count) or should the development process be considered? A better development process might introduce fewer faults to be discovered by testing and suggest that the customer should choose the product with the lower fault count. In reality it is impossible to decide, given this limited amount of information. Detailed information on the entire process of product construction and the technologies utilized is required for the customer to make an informed choice.

2.2.2 Difficulties in data collection

It may be more than a fear of lost business that dissuades software developers from releasing fault data. There are a number of practical difficulties associated with collecting this type of data. It is very hard to collect information pertaining to faults automatically so this means that developers have to fill in forms for each fault found. This may be done with a reasonable amount of accuracy during the earlier stages of the project when the developers are not under too much pressure. However, in the testing and integration stages (when you would expect large numbers of faults to be uncovered), the project is nearing completion, the delivery date is getting closer and there is usually tremendous pressure on the developers to complete the work as fast as possible. It is frequently observed that if a project schedule is slipping then it is often the testing stage that suffers. If someone is under pressure to test a product as quickly as possible then the last thing they are going to want to do is to sit down and carefully fill in a form for each fault found in the product. Therefore, unless a project is extremely well managed, it is often difficult to get reliable data from manual collection methods.

2.2.3 Why classify?

Given the complex relationship that exists between errors, faults and failures it is easy to see that the production of a general classification scheme or taxonomy is not going to be a trivial task. Indeed there are those who oppose such a scheme. Myers (1976), for instance, argues against the classification of faults on the grounds that it focuses on manifestations rather than the original causes. He argues that data showing that, for example, '29 per cent of all errors are found in IF statements' do not help in the task of eliminating errors. This is fair comment and serves to emphasize the importance of defining the purpose of any classification scheme.

Bowen (1980) gives an excellent summary of some of the earlier studies and argues for the classification of the data collected on the following grounds. It should:

- Provide feedback to develop software design standards.
- Provide guidance to test engineers.
- Evaluate modern programming practices.
- Evaluate verification and validation tools.
- Validate and support quantitative reliability models.

He further argues that good use could be made of a history base of projects which (recognizing the difficulties of comparison due to different programmer background, software and hardware environments, applications, etc.), for example, may show that similar software exhibits similar faults and so software producers may benefit from using tools and techniques that have shown themselves to be effective.

In addition, classification encourages the development of test methods that are directed at particular kinds of faults (many of the more recently developed methods are based on this notion) and the meaningful comparison of test methods. This, in turn, provides testers with more information on which methods to employ and so enables them to choose a portfolio of complementary techniques likely to expose that largest number of faults.

2.2.4 Should we classify failures?

Beizer (1983) puts forward a ten-point scale of failures which starts at mild (e.g. aesthetic offence), and moves through the disturbing (e.g. refuses to handle legitimate transactions), and the very serious (e.g. system does the wrong transaction), to the infectious (e.g. erodes the social or physical environment). He also points out that all of the ten categories could have arisen from exactly the same fault (the example used is a bit being set rather than reset). What is more, depending on the way that the system is being used, it is possible that the system could have produced all categories of failure at different times.

These factors make the categorization of failures difficult but, as Beizer argues, it is valuable for software developers to see the consequences of their actions. It is easy for the programmer to hide behind the fault—there sounds nothing too terrible about an unset bit—but exposure to the possible failures that might have followed can be a sobering experience. However, this can also have detrimental effects. Software developers might try to hide faults and the situation whereby mistakes are covered up may dominate—precisely the kind of situation that should be avoided if a healthy and effective testing environment is to survive. Furthermore, the classification of failures may not be feasible. For example, if a fault is found during the early stages of testing when the system is incomplete, it may be impossible to state what the consequences are (the behaviour of the system may not be completely defined at that stage).

There are times when the classification of failures is particularly useful. During systems testing, shortly before the product is to be shipped to the customer, it is inevitable that a number of failures will be noticed. It is also inevitable that there will simply not be the time to fix every single fault that causes these failures and so some criterion has to be brought in to determine which faults should be fixed and which deferred until a later date. One criterion might be ease of fix, or ease of identification of fault (since time is limited). A less short-sighted alternative is gravity of failure. Users of software have got used to putting up with 'little idiosyncrasies' such as incorrectly formatted output, or commands that require the system to be in a particular mode before they will work. They tend to work their way around these. But once the system begins doing some damage, be it real in terms of corrupting data, or otherwise in terms of producing incorrect results, then that system will quickly fall out of use. For this reason the classification of failures is beneficial in trying to ensure that the failures that are going to occur will at least be minor in nature and tolerable (albeit temporarily) by the user.

The classification of failures is also beneficial in performing any kind of reliability assessment. Reliability assessment looks at failure data (when they occurred during the operation of a system) and attempts to fit a model to these data which may then be used to do such things as determine the rate of failure and predict the time to the next failure. Given two similar systems, both of which have the same rates of failure but one produces output which is aesthetically displeasing and the other endangers human life, then in pragmatic terms it is clear that they are not equivalently reliable.

2.3 STUDIES OF ERRORS, FAULTS AND FAILURES

In this section the main results of some of the more comprehensive studies made over the past 20 years are described. I am aware that several pages of summarized experiments do not necessarily make for exciting reading. The main difficulty is that, for the very reasons discussed in the earlier sections of this chapter, all the experiments and studies have different characteristics, or use different fault classifications, or are based on different types of software, or use different testing strategies, or . . . the list goes on. As a consequence, each study has to be dealt with individually.

2.3.1 The studies

Endres (1975)

This looked at faults discovered during the internal testing of the DOS/VS operating system. This led to a database of problems of which 432 were regarded as programming errors. An interesting point is the definition of a fault as the correction being made. It is pointed out that sometimes, if the fault lies too deep, it may be too expensive to effect a total cure and so the correction may be 'simpler' than the actual fault. Also, the number of faults was equated to the number of problems. However, as Endres points out, sometimes the same fault caused several problems.

The notable results from this study showed that the vast majority of modules contained only one fault. Furthermore the faults tended to affect a small number of modules, which seems to suggest that integration faults were not a problem in this study (although the validity of this conclusion could be questioned since it depends on the interpretation of the word 'affect'—it is only necessary to have a fault in one module for an integration fault to occur). Endres goes on to point out that the three modules containing the largest number of faults were by far the largest (more than 3000 instructions), and the fourth 'most faulty' module was one that was extremely unstable.

Endres went on to group the faults into three classes: those relating to the solving of the problem (which in turn had subclasses such as *machine configuration and architecture*, *functions offered*, and *output listings and formats*) which contained 46 per cent of the faults, those relating to the implementation (e.g. *reference to names*, *counting and calculating*) which contained 38 per cent of the faults, and others (e.g. *spelling errors*, *missing commentaries*) which contained the remaining 16 per cent. The first two categories were further subdivided to give classes of fault which are highly application-specific.

Rubey et al. *(1975)*

This study (which looked at small real-time programs developed by experienced staff) makes a distinction between faults found in the course of validation efforts and those found during the normal development activity. It found that during development the rate of faults was about one per ten lines of machine language instruction. This falls to around two faults per 1000 lines of machine language instructions during validation. The development process itself found around 98 per cent of faults, leaving only 2 per cent to be found by validation; the suggestion being that validation needed something rather special in the way of tools and techniques to find these faults.

The faults discovered were put into ten categories and their associated failures ranked (according to the initial effect of the failure) as serious, moderate or minor. By far the largest number of faults were those falling into the *incomplete or erroneous specification* (28 per cent) category, but these were mostly of a minor nature. Those that were most problematic (in that they composed the majority of serious or moderate faults) were those

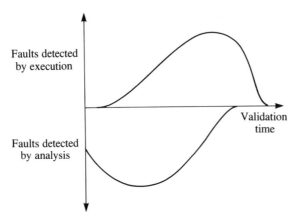

Figure 2.2 Effectiveness of analysis and execution methods in validation stage (© 1975, IEEE).

in the categories of *erroneous decision logic or sequencing* (12 per cent), *erroneous data accessing* (10 per cent), *erroneous arithmetic computations* (9 per cent) and *intentional deviation from specification* (12 per cent).

The faults detected by analysis methods and execution methods were also compared, with execution methods finding about 25 per cent more faults than analysis methods. However, as is shown in Fig. 2.2, the analysis methods were seen to be more effective in the earlier stages of validation.

Schneidewind and Hoffman (1979)

Four small projects written in Algol W were investigated. The size of the projects meant that there was little in the way of requirements analysis or system integration. Prior to the study, five fault categories were defined: *design, coding, clerical, debugging* and *testing*. (In an attempt to be consistent, I have frequently renamed 'error' as 'fault'. Most of the time this does not lead to any problems—in this example a subcategory of *coding* is an 'initialization error' which may simply be read as 'initialization fault' without any loss of meaning. However, there are also instances where confusion can occur. Again in this example, there is a subcategory of clerical called 'mental error'. To simply rename this as 'mental fault' would be wrong since it *is* trying to describe an error. The problem is that the distinction was not made between faults and errors when the categories were defined. As a solution (and not an ideal one), I feel it is best to examine the faults (since this can give us the most information) and to ignore the errors as being beyond the current technology and scope of this book.)

These five fault categories are further broken down into 17 and 31 subcategories respectively in the cases of design and coding. However, this is

Table 2.1 Number and percentage of faults according to categories

Category of fault	Number of faults	Percentage of total (approx.)
Design	35	20.2
Coding	97	56.1
Clerical	37	21.4
Debugging	4	2.3

Source: Schneidewind and Hoffman (1979) (© 1979, IEEE).

too detailed for our purposes so we will remain with the five major categories. The summary results from the investigation are presented in Table 2.1. The testing fault category is missing from the results. It would appear that no faults of this nature were encountered, although this is not clear.

It should be noted that the high number of coding faults in Table 2.1 is partially attributable to the inclusion of faults in syntax. They went on to study the faults further and found that of the original 173, 64 were found during the debugging and testing phases. Unfortunately, no further analysis of these faults is presented. The most common individual fault fell into the class of manual faults and is defined as a manual error which 'could result from lack of motor skill or temporary manual dysfunction . . .'!

Glass (1981)

The software problem reports from two large embedded software projects were collected and 100 reports (which were attributable to software faults) from each project examined in detail (see Table 2.2 for the main findings of

Table 2.2 Percentage of faults according to categories

Category of fault	Percentage of total (approx.)
Omitted logic	31.9
Failure to reset data	12.2
Regression fault	9.0
Documentation at fault	8.5
Requirements inadequate	5.9
Patch at fault	5.9
Commentary at fault	5.9
IF statement too simple	5.9
Referenced wrong data variable	5.3
Data alignment fault	3.7
Timing fault causes data loss	3.2
Failure to initialize data	2.7

Source: (Glass (1981) (© 1981, IEEE).

the study). No classification scheme was chosen; instead the faults were allowed to 'self-classify'. In other words, a problem report was either assigned to its own new category or to one that already existed. Glass also included another category for all those faults that totalled four or less.

As may be seen, the category of *omitted logic* dominates the findings. Glass observes that these are instances of the software not being complex enough for the problem. He also goes on to suggest that 'these problems of complexity may be considered to be design errors, and indeed many of them are'. However, they are errors that exist at a fuzzy level between design and code and it is Glass's feeling that to label them as design errors would be too simplistic.

This paper also contains my favourite example of a software problem report. The explanation given for the problem is 'Insufficient brain power applied during design'.

Werner (1986)

Software correction notices were reviewed relating to eight production data processing systems written in COBOL. These revealed 188 faults which were then classified according to the scheme proposed by Howden (1982a) with the addition of a class to represent *clerical faults*. The results are shown in Table 2.3. The table demonstrates that the class of logic faults dominates the results. These logical faults consisted of such things as *missing cases* (i.e. data for which there is no logic), *logical operations out of sequence*, *missing or wrong*, and *missing conditions* (pieces of compound expression absent).

Ostrand and Weyuker (1984)

Problems from a special-purpose editor project consisting of around 10 000 lines of high-level code and 1000 lines of assembler were recorded on a Software User Report form. The symptoms of the problem were described

Table 2.3 Number of faults according to categories

Category of fault	Number
Clerical	15
Computation	13
Data declaration	15
Interface	6
Data reference	13
Input/output	24
Logic	102

Source: Werner (1986) (reproduced with kind permission of the ACM).

with no attempt at classification made at this stage. In addition, direct questions were asked to try and determine the error made to cause the fault.

A fault is described using an attribute classification scheme. That is, a fault is not ascribed to a single category but has a number of attributes recorded about it. It is argued that this scheme is easily extensible (attributes may be added) and will undoubtedly grow as more studies are made. The attributes at the time of the study were:

- *Major category*—Data Definition (constants, storage areas, etc.), Data Handling (initialization and manipulation), Decision, Decision and Processing (as a direct consequence of the decision being true), Documentation, System and Not an Error.
- *Type*—If the fault involved data, this describes its type.
- *Presence*—Was the fault due to omitted, superfluous or incorrect code.
- *Use*—Operations being performed in a data handling fault.

Another interesting point illustrated by Ostrand and Weyuker is that one fault may lead to several different classifications (i.e. the categories are not mutually exclusive).

Initially 171 forms were examined of which 15 were rejected because they were mistakes of a clerical nature. The remaining 156 were analysed and in 15 cases a report described two faults, and in one case a report described three faults. This accounts for a total of 173 faults. They found that the majority of faults were discovered in the testing stages (as opposed to design, coding or system testing stages) with 30 per cent of faults being found at the unit testing stage and 61 per cent at the function testing stage. It should be noted that the function testing was carried out by an independent body which may account for the success of this process. The categorization of faults is shown in Table 2.4.

Table 2.4 Number of faults and percentages according to categories

Category of fault	Number	Percentage
Data definition	56	32
Data handling	38	22
Decision and processing	32	18
Decision (alone)	31	18
System	12	7
Documentation	2	1
Unknown	2	1

Further investigation was carried out to determine how the faults were detected. The interesting results from this reveal that unit testing was only really effective in terms of detecting data handling faults (finding just over 50 per cent of the faults) and reasonably effective in detecting decision faults (finding around 30 per cent). Functional testing, on the other hand, detected nearly 90 per cent of data definition faults, about 30 per cent of data handling faults, 75 per cent of decision plus processing faults and 60 per cent of decision faults. A suggested reason for this is that problems in specifications (ambiguity, lack of clarity, etc.) were cited as the cause of 41 per cent of the decision plus processing faults, 19 per cent of the decision faults, 18 per cent of the data definition faults but only 3 per cent of the data handling faults. The independent perspective of function testing is bound to be more effective when there are problems with the specification. The programmer has had to interpret the specification one way in order to code it and is unlikely to interpret it a different way to test it.

The faults were further analysed to determine if they were faults of *omission* (e.g. part of a decision or operation is missing) or faults of *commission* (e.g. the wrong operator is used or the coding is in some similar way incorrect—but present). These findings are summarized in Table 2.5. It should be noted that the Data Handling category also included 5 per cent superfluous code faults (i.e. there is more code than necessary to handle the problem, or the system is doing more than required).

Ostrand and Weyuker point out that the large number of faults of omission is an important message to testers. Techniques that rely solely on analysis of implemented code are unlikely to be successful in finding faults due to absent code. It places the emphasis on using those techniques that are based on the specification, design or requirements documents. It is also shown that faults of this nature take longer to fix because new code needs to be created rather than existing code changed.

Table 2.5 Percentage of faults of commission and omission according to categories

Category of fault	Percentage of faults of commission	Percentage of faults of omission
Data definition	68	32
Data handling	50	45
Decision (alone)	35	65
Decision and processing	3	97

Reprinted by permission of the publisher from 'Collecting and categorizing software error data in an industrial environment' by Thomas J. Ostrand and Elaine J. Weyuker, *The Journal of Systems and Software*, **4** (4), 289–300 (© 1984, Elsevier Science Publishing Co., Inc.).

Analysis of the reasons for the errors occurring revealed a tendency for programmers to blame themselves. This self-flagellating tendency persisted through further analysis until it came to omitted code faults, when they were happier to lay the problem at the feet of the specification. Inadequate specifications were cited as the reason for 12 per cent of the errors—this being the second most common cause.

Basili and Perricone (1984)

A system for general satellite planning studies consisting of 90 000 lines of FORTRAN (with a large number of reused modules) was studied at the Software Engineering Laboratory. Change report forms totalling 231 and produced over 33 months were examined. They contained details of the reason for, and description of, change, the type of change, the type of fault (if applicable) and the validation activities used for detection. The number of modules affected by a fault is shown in Table 2.6. It should be noted that

Table 2.6   Number of modules affected by a fault

Number of faults	Number of modules affected
155	1
9	2
3	3
6	4
1	5

Source: Basili and Perricone (reproduced with kind permission of the ACM).

Table 2.7   Number of faults per module

Number of modules	New	Modified	Number of faults per module
36	17	19	1
26	13	13	2
16	10	6	3
13	7	6	4
4	1	3	5
1	1	—	7

Source: Basili and Perricone (reproduced with kind permission of the ACM).

Basili and Perricone use what at first seems a slightly idiosyncratic method of counting faults and so the total number of faults may differ between tables.

Table 2.7 shows the number of faults per module and makes a further distinction between new modules and modified modules (those that are the subject of reuse).

The most fault-prone modules in both categories were analysed further and it was found that almost all faults were attributable to two categories: *misunderstood or incorrect specifications*, or *incorrect design or implementation of a module component*. The sources of the faults (in other words, the errors) were investigated and the major causes were found to be *functional specification incorrect or misinterpreted* (36 per cent) followed by *mistake in control logic or computation of an expression (single component)* (16 per cent), and *requirements incorrect or misinterpreted* and *clerical error* (12 per cent).

The faults were further subjected to an additional classification. This 'abstract' classification consisted of five types of fault:

- *Initialization*—failure to initialize or re-initialize a data structure upon entering or leaving a module.
- *Control*—cause an incorrect path to be followed.
- *Interface*—faults associated with structures existing outside the module's local environment.
- *Data*—incorrect use of data structure (e.g. subscript, variable, etc.).
- *Computation*—incorrect evaluation of an expression.

These five categories were further partitioned into faults of omission and commission. The results are shown in Table 2.8.

Table 2.8 Abstract fault classification

Classification	Commission		Omission	
	New	Modified	New	Modified
Initialization	2	9	5	9
Control	12	2	16	28
Interface	23	31	27	6
Data	10	17	1	3
Computation	16	21	3	3

Source: Basili and Perricone (reproduced with kind permission of the ACM).

2.3.2 Implications for the tester

Bearing in mind that the above studies involved different developers in different environments producing different software, it is unreasonable to subject the data to any statistical analysis. However, some general trends emerge from the studies and it is beneficial to note these. The general picture of faults in software is:

- A large number of modules will have a small number of faults.
- A small number of modules will have a large number of faults.
- A large number of faults affect a small number of modules.
- A small number of faults affect a large number of modules.
- Omitted logic (the implementation being unable to cope with all of the specification) is a prevalent and persistent fault.
- Faults related to data are more frequent than those related to computation.
- Interface faults and integration faults need further study.
- Apart from human error, specifications are a common cause of fault.

Several of these point to the benefit of using an independent functional testing team.

2.3.3 Hints on data collection

The conclusions in the previous section are tentatively based on a handful of studies. More studies are needed and more good experimental work needs to be carried out (this also goes for most other areas of software engineering). It is important that a similar classification scheme is employed for future studies to allow as much comparison as possible (given the unknown variables that will exist—environment, product type, programmer skill, etc.). From the later studies, a general picture emerges of the major categories of fault. Given the experience of those studies and the fact that they are very informative, there seems little point in departing significantly from their approach. It is also useful to have more than a one-dimensional categorization. So, in addition to the major fault category, information such as the type of data involved (if appropriate), and whether it is a fault involving omitted, superfluous or incorrect code, is very useful.

Ultimately, the type of data collected depends upon what is going to be done with it. There is no point in collecting data that are not going to be used. Similarly, it is essential to decide beforehand what kind of information is required from the data and ensure that the appropriate data are collected. For example, if it is information on comparing test methods that is required, then it is vital to record the test method that generated the data that revealed the fault. It is no use trying to add in information of this nature retrospectively.

One feature of the studies that were looked at in the previous section was that they tended to look at faults in the *code*. The reasons for doing this are obvious, but it is also well known that faults are expensive to repair once they get this far. It is important to try to detect (and correct) faults as soon as they are found. This suggests that it is beneficial to try to detect the source of faults and use this information to employ techniques that will detect faults earlier in the development stages.

3

TESTING METHODS

3.1 INTRODUCTION

The aim of this chapter is to provide a description of the existing testing techniques. When I say 'existing' I am aware that new techniques are constantly being developed and some older ones are undergoing revision, so this represents a snapshot of those methods that were 'ripe' at the time of writing. Testing researchers are frequently criticized for their work being inaccessible to the everyday software developer. This is by no means suggesting that the average programmer is an intellectual pygmy. It is acknowledging that time is a precious resource, and the pressure of developing software to tight schedules does not often allow it to be squandered on finding and studying a research paper, report or conference proceedings. I have therefore taken a very practical view of the testing techniques and have attempted to present them in a way that a programmer may find concise and helpful (my apologies to any researcher who feels that their 'pet' method has been misrepresented as a consequence of this treatment!). In addition, I hope that the methods have been presented in a way that is beneficial to researchers in testing and software engineering.

In making the approach practical I have chosen to demonstrate the application of the techniques to the specification and program shown in Fig. 3.1. In using this example I am aware that any professional programmer will scoff at this program and regard it as being almost too trivial to bother with.

```
(* Specification:                                                  *)
(* The program prompts the user for a positive integer in the      *)
(* range 1 to 20 and then for a string of characters of that length. *)
(* The program then prompts for a character and returns the position *)
(* in the string at which the character was first found or a message *)
(* indicating that the character was not present in the string. The *)
(* user has the option to search for more characters.              *)

1    program example(input, output);
2    var a : array[1 .. 20] of char;
3        x,i: integer;
4        c, response: char;
5        found: boolean;
6    begin
7      writeln('Input an integer between 1 and 20');
8      readln(x);
9    while (x < 1) or (x > 20) do
10     begin
11       writeln('Input an integer between 1 and 20');
12       readln(x)
13     end;
14     writeln('input ',x,' characters');
15     for i := 1 to x do
16        read(a[i]);
17     readln;
18     repeat
19       writeln('Input character to be searched for: ');
20       readln(c);
21       found := FALSE;
22       i := 1;
23       while (not(found)) and (i <= x) do
24         begin
25           if a[i] = c then
26               found := TRUE
27           else
28               i := i +1
29         end;
30         if found then
31            writeln('Character ',c,' appears at position',i)
32         else
33            writeln('Character ',c,' does not occur in the string');
34         writeln;
35         writeln('Search for another character? [y/n]');
36         readln(response);
37     until (response = 'n') or (response = 'N');
38   end.
```

Figure 3.1 Example program used to demonstrate application of testing methods.

In its defence I must point out that it was developed specifically to demonstrate the application of a large number of testing methods in a realistic amount of space. To do this requires a small program with a variety of control and logical constructions written in an imperative language (most methods are developed with imperative languages in mind—the choice of Pascal was quite arbitrary) with a natural language specification. Line numbers have been added for reference purposes. This quickly leads to the horribly contrived example used in this text! This example is inadequate for some methods and the descriptions of these are furnished with more appropriate ones.

Each method is described in a similar way with the following sections:

- *Name*
- *Description*—Steps involved in using the method (what to do).
- *Application*—Application of the method to the example (how to do it). Example of data generated.
- *Strengths/weaknesses*—Short evaluation of the method.
- *References*—Principal references for further details.

3.2 THE METHODS

3.2.1 Statement testing

Description

Generate test data to execute every source language statement in the program at least once. Also referred to as statement coverage.

Application

In order to achieve statement coverage we need to be concerned about those statements that are controlled by conditions. So, initially, we have to supply a value of x which is out of range to force the execution of statements in the loop (lines 11–12). As long as x is at least 1 (which it will be) the statement inside the *for*-loop (line 16) will be executed. The *if*-statement (line 25) needs to be executed (entry to the *while*-loop is guaranteed) as well as the *true* and *false* outcomes (lines 26 and 28). This means that we have to find a character successfully and move along the array as a consequence of not finding the character. *True* and *false* outcomes for the *if*-statement (line 30) also need to be generated. Again this means one successful and one unsuccessful character match. This requirement can be combined with the requirement for the previous *if*-statement to yield test data that consist of an array, *a* of one character and values for *c* that occur in *a* and don't occur in *a*. Finally we need to exit the repeat loop to execute the final *end* statement (line 38).

This leads to the minimal set of test data shown in Table 3.1.

Strengths and weaknesses

Statement testing is usually regarded as the minimum level of coverage to be achieved using structural testing. This is based on the feeling that it is absurd to release a piece of software without having executed every statement.

Table 3.1 Test data for statement testing

Input				Expected output
x	a	c	response	
25 1	x	x a	y n	Input an integer between 1 and 20 Character x appears at position 1 Character a does not occur in the string

However, it is acknowledged that frequently it is impossible to achieve 100 per cent statement coverage. This is usually due to the presence of pieces of code or routines that are only executed in exceptional circumstances (for example, error routines or exception handlers) which are very hard, or even dangerous, to reproduce. Such routines, if impossible to test, should at least be subjected to rigorous inspection procedures. It is then reasonable to discount them when examining the coverage achieved by statement testing. Further inhibitors to 100 per cent statement testing is the existence of unreachable, or 'island', code. This is code that cannot be executed by any combination of input data and is symptomatic of a design error or poor maintenance. Such code should either be made reachable if it is needed, or removed.

The strength of statement testing is that it does force the execution of every statement. However, it is not very demanding in its execution, particularly when it comes to compound logical conditions. For example, we did not generate any value of x that was less than 1 to test the first condition in the *while*-loop (line 9). Further problems occur when we encounter constructs like the 'null else' situation illustrated below:

.
.
.

```
if Num < 3 then
   Num := Num + 7;
```

.
.

Statement testing will force the execution of the *true* part of the *if*-statement but, because there is no *else* part, will not demand that data be generated to force a *false* outcome.

Lesniak-Betley (1984) describes an investigation into the effectiveness of statement testing. The technique was extended to cope with the 'null else' problem described above and then a count of the faults discovered was made. Test data were then generated for a subset of the modules using a technique called input analysis which generates combinations of input test data. The input analysis technique generated far more data than the statement testing but found only two more faults. This would seem to suggest that it is not worth investing in the extra effort to generate more data than those generated by statement testing. However, this needs some examination on two counts. Firstly, even though the input analysis technique generated much more data, there is no reason to assume that the data were much more rigorous or demanding than those generated by statement testing. Secondly, the software was a conversion project and the old code acted as a specification for the new. This suggests that the problem was quite well defined and there were unlikely to be many faults occurring as a consequence of the specification being poor or misunderstood.

References

It may be as a result of the perceived simplicity of the subject, but there are few references on statement testing. It is briefly dealt with by Myers (1979), Adrion *et al.* (1982), Prather (1983), and Ould and Unwin (1986).

3.2.2 Branch testing

This is also referred to as branch coverage or decision coverage.

Description

Generate test data to exercise the *true and false* outcomes of every decision.

Application

When carrying out branch testing it is frequently convenient to examine the directed graph representation of the program (in many ways similar to a conventional flowchart) which shows the flow of control through the program using a network of nodes and edges. A node represents a block of code (a sequence of statements such that if the first statement is executed then so are all other statements) and an edge represents the transfer of control (the *true* and *false* outcomes of an *if*-statement, for example). The directed graph contains no information on the conditions that control the branching or the statements being executed. It is purely an abstraction used to examine the structure of the program. For a more formal treatment of directed graphs, see Huang (1975) and Prather (1983).

The directed graph of the example program is shown in Fig. 3.2. The nodes are numbered and the edges labelled for reference purposes. The numbers within the nodes are the program line numbers represented by that node (usually, directed graphs carry no such information).

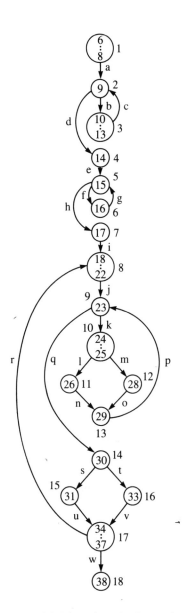

Figure 3.2 Directed graph of example program.

With reference to the graph, the branches for which we have to generate test data to cause *true* and *false* outcomes occur at nodes 2, 5, 9, 10, 14 and 17.

For node 2 a value of *x* less than 1 or greater than 20 will cause the *true* branch (b) to be taken, and a value of *x* within these limits will cause the false branch to be taken (d).

Node 5 represents the *for*-loop which will have *true* and *false* outcomes as long as *x* is at least 1 (which it will be).

For node 9, entry to the *while*-loop (a *true* outcome—edge k) is guaranteed (due to the statements on lines 21 and 22), and a *false* outcome (q) by either finding the character being searched for or reaching the end of the string.

Node 10 relates to the *if*-statement (line 25) which requires a successful comparison with the character in the string (l, n) and a failed comparison to cause *i* to be incremented (m, o).

Node 14 demands that one character is found in the string and one character is not found in the string.

Node 17 requires us to make at least one more traversal of the *repeat*-loop before terminating the program.

This leads to the set of test data shown in Table 3.2.

Table 3.2 Test data for branch testing

Input				Expected output
x	*a*	*c*	*response*	
25				Input an integer between 1 and 20
1	x	x		Character x appears at position 1
			y	
		a		Character a does not occur in the string
			n	

It is worth noting that in this case branch testing is satisfied by exactly the same test data as those required by statement testing. This is not normally the case, and need not have been for the following reason: statement testing required us to find a character in the string and fail to find a character in the string, and we chose to do this using the *repeat*-loop. This was not necessary and we could just as well have executed the program again with the other set of test data—it was purely convenience that drove us to use the *repeat*-loop. Branch testing, on the other hand, demands that the *repeat*-loop be exercised in this fashion.

Strengths and weaknesses

Branch testing is regarded as the next level up from statement testing (and suffers from the same problems when trying to achieve 100 per cent coverage—as do all such structural testing methods) since it resolves the 'null else' problem by forcing the *true* and *false* outcomes of each branch, even if there is no code associated with these outcomes.

Its weakness is in the testing of compound conditions—it is quite undemanding of the conditions guarding a branch. For example, given the following situation:

.

.

.

```
if A = "X" or ( B < 0.0012 and C = TRUE and
  (D >= 112 or E = "Yes")) then
  { some code }
else
  { some more code}
```

.

.

All we have to do to achieve a true outcome is to give A a value of X. We don't have to bother about the rest of the condition.

References

Further information may be found in Myers (1979), Prather (1983), and Ould and Unwin (1986). An interesting investigation of branch testing coverage levels is provided by Chusho (1983), who applies a reduction algorithm to the directed graph to give a more representative coverage ratio. See also DD-path (Sec. 3.2.3 below). Another interesting approach to achieving branch coverage is the *path prefix* testing strategy as described in Prather and Myers (1987). This is an example of an *adaptive testing method* whereby new paths through a program are tested by modifying the data used to test already-covered paths. The idea is to test only one new path (or branch) at a time, using the existing data as a guide to create the test data to cover this new path. The program under test is initially executed with some arbitrary set of data. The branches covered by these data are noted and then the first branch whose condition may be reversed, and which will add a new branch, is chosen. The input data are then modified to cause the reversal of this condition and hence the execution of a new branch. The process is continued until total branch coverage is achieved.

3.2.3 DD-path

Description

A DD-path (or, to give it its full name, decision-to-decision path) is, as is implied, a path between decisions. It is a subpath of a graph which begins either at the start node (the first node in a graph) or a decision node. It finishes either at the end node or at a decision node and must contain no decision nodes within it (other than those at either end).

Application

Applying the definition above, the DD-paths for the example are as follows (the numbers represent the node numbers):

1. 1–2
2. 2–3–2
3. 2–4–5
4. 5–6–5
5. 5–7–8–9
6. 9–10
7. 10–11–13–9
8. 10–12–13–9
9. 9–14
10. 14–15–17
11. 14–16–17
12. 17–8–9
13. 17–18

A testing goal for DD-paths is to aim to cover all DD-paths at least once. That is, we have to generate test data to force execution of all of the subpaths listed above. This is equivalent to branch testing (and thus the same test data would achieve coverage of all DD-paths).

Strengths and weaknesses

As for branch testing.

References

The topic of DD-paths is covered in Prather (1983) and Woodward (1984). Chusho (1983) has written an interesting paper based on the idea that when the coverage ratio is less than 100 per cent the ratio of executed paths to total DD-paths is greater than the ratio of executed test data to all test data. That is, the coverage ratio is not a true reflection of work done. The concept of an essential branch is defined (which ignores a previously covered DD-path) and a graph reduction algorithm is applied to achieve a more linear coverage ratio.

3.2.4 Condition coverage

This may also be referred to as condition testing.

Description

Generate test data such that all conditions in a decision take on both outcomes (if possible) at least once.

Application

Again we have to consider all the nodes identified by branch testing, but this time we need to look at all the conditions within the decisions at the nodes.

Considering the first *while*-loop—a decision with two conditions:

```
while (x < 1) or (x > 20) do
```

Supplying test data values of 0 and 21 for x would achieve condition coverage: $x = 0$ causes the first condition to be evaluated to *true* and the second to *false*, and $x = 21$ causes the first condition to be evaluated to *false* and the second to *true*. However, we need to generate a further value of x which falls within the limits so as to allow the execution of the rest of the program. We shall let this value be determined by the requirements imposed by conditions occurring later in the program.

The next condition to consider is that in the *for*-loop:

```
for i := 1 to x do
```

Some people might question the treatment of such a construct using condition coverage. Termination of the loop is guaranteed and it may not be immediately obvious what the condition is. However, these points may just be a feature of Pascal. If we examine the construct in other languages, say for example, C:

```
for (i = 1; i <= x; i++)
```

or COBOL:

```
perform paragraph-name varying i from 1 by i until i > x.
```

then the condition becomes more obvious. For a *true* outcome *i* must be less than or equal to x and for a *false* outcome *i* must be greater than x. Since x is at least 1 we have to enter the *for*-loop and then increment *i* until it is greater than x—exactly the same as we did in statement and branch testing—by reading in x characters.

Next we have to consider the *while*-loop at line 23 (node 9). Both conditions within this decision will be *true* on entry to the loop. To cause them to be evaluated to *false*, we need to successfully find a character and fail to find the character (i.e. cause *i* to be incremented beyond the value of x). This will also generate *true* and *false* outcomes for the *if*-statements at lines 25 and 30.

The final decision to consider is the *until*-statement at line 37 (node 17) which reads:

```
until (response = 'n') or (response = 'N');
```

Supplying *response* with a value of 'n' will cause the first condition to be *true* and the second to be *false*. Supplying *response* with a value of 'N' will reverse this situation and achieve condition coverage. To achieve this we will need to execute the program twice.

The test data necessary to achieve condition coverage are shown in Table 3.3. Note that values for the second set of data are shown below the double horizontal line.

Table 3.3 Test data for condition coverage

Input				Expected output
x	a	c	*response*	
21				Input an integer between 1 and 20
0				Input an integer between 1 and 20
1	x	x		Character x appears at position 1
			n	
1	x	a		Character a does not occur in the string
			N	

Strengths and weaknesses

The strength of condition testing is that it does focus on conditions within decisions in a way that techniques like branch testing do not. A drawback is that it may fail to achieve branch coverage. This is demonstrated in the data generated for our example. The *repeat*-loop is only executed once by each set of test data and a *false* outcome (edge r in the graph) is never exercised.

References

Further information may be found in Myers (1979), Prather (1983), and Ould and Unwin (1986).

3.2.5 Decision/condition coverage

This may also be referred to as decision/condition testing.

Description

Generate test data such that all conditions in a decision take on both outcomes (if possible) at least once, and exercise the *true* and *false* outcomes of every decision.

Application

Decision/condition coverage is a combination of condition coverage and decision coverage (or branch testing). It is necessary to generate the same test data as for condition coverage but also to ensure that each branch or decision takes a *true* and *false* outcome. This means that we need to modify the test data generated by condition testing to include a value of 'y' (or anything else other than 'n' or 'N') to exercise the false branch (edge r) of the *repeat . . . until*-loop.

The test data necessary to achieve decision/condition coverage are shown in Table 3.4. Note that values for the second set of data (shown below the double horizontal line) are quite arbitrary. All we are concerned with is generating a value of 'N' for *response*.

Table 3.4 Test data for decision/condition coverage

Input				Expected output
x	*a*	*c*	*response*	
21				Input an integer between 1 and 20
0				Input an integer between 1 and 20
1	x	x		Character x appears at position 1
			y	
		a		Character a does not occur in the string
			n	
1	x	a		Character a does not occur in the string
			N	

Strengths and weaknesses

Decision/condition coverage makes up for one of the main deficiencies of condition coverage by forcing each branch to take a *true* and *false* outcome. One possible weakness is that conditions can be masked due to the potential lazy evaluation of compound conditions. Given the *while*-statement in the example:

```
while (not(found)) and (i <= x)
```

For the entire decision to be *true*, both conditions need to be evaluated to *true*. For the decision to be *false*, only the first condition needs to be evaluated to *false*. The consequence is that we might not have exercised the consequence of the second condition having a *false* outcome.

References

Further information may be found in Myers (1979), Prather (1983), and Ould and Unwin (1986).

3.2.6 Multiple condition coverage

This may also be referred to as multiple condition testing.

Description

Generate test data to exercise all possible combinations of *true* and *false* outcomes of conditions within a decision.

Application

This does not affect the simple decisions in the program (except in that they may need to handle any extra data generated as a consequence) so it is only necessary to examine the compound conditions at lines 9, 23 and 37.

Considering line 9 which has the decision:

```
while (x < 1) or (x > 20)
```

This may be represented as a sort of truth table showing the outcomes of the conditions and test data that would cause this outcome. This representation is shown in Table 3.5.

Similarly the representations for the compounded conditions on lines 23 and 37 are shown in Tables 3.6 and 3.7.

It is worth pointing out that in this example, all three cases had a combination of conditions for which it was impossible to generate test data—this is by no means normally the case. In this case the combined set of final test data turns out to be the same as that required for decision/condition coverage.

Table 3.5 Multiple condition coverage for decision on line 9

(x < 1)	or	(x > 20)	Test data
T		T	Impossible
T		F	$x = 0$
F		T	$x = 21$
F		F	$x = 1$

Table 3.6 Multiple condition coverage for decision on line 23

(not(found)) and (i <= x)		Test requirements
T	T	*True* on entry
T	F	Character not found in string
F	T	Character found in string
F	F	Impossible

Table 3.7 Multiple condition coverage for decision on line 37

(response = 'n') or (response = 'N')		Test data
T	T	Impossible
T	F	'n'
F	T	'N'
F	F	'y' (or anything but 'n' or 'N')

Strengths and weaknesses

The main strength of multiple condition coverage is that it does test all feasible combinations of outcomes of each condition, thereby giving confidence in the Boolean operators used to compound the conditions.

A drawback is that no assistance is given in the choice of test data. For example, when choosing a value for x that is less than 1, then -4123 would have been an equally valid choice as 0. This is true of all structural methods of this kind.

Furthermore, multiple condition coverage is expensive (with structural testing the general rule is that the higher the coverage, the more test data is required and hence the more the method costs to apply). In the example, there is a maximum of two conditions in any decision. Most programs involve many more complex decisions. For multiple condition coverage, a decision involving n conditions will have 2^n combinations and thus require a maximum of 2^n test cases.

References

Further information may be found in Myers (1979), Prather (1983), and Ould and Unwin (1986).

3.2.7 Level-i paths

Description

A *level-0* path is a simple acyclic (i.e. there are no circuits or loops in it) path from the start node to the stop node of a graph. A *level-i* path (for values of i

greater than 0) is a path that begins and ends on the nodes of a lower level and may be a circuit (in that it begins and ends on the same node). Typically, level-i paths (when i is at least 1) represent nested loops. Level-i paths are used to guide an incremental testing strategy that generates test data firstly to cover all level-0 paths, then all level-1 paths (accessing them through the level-0 paths), followed by all level-2 paths, and so on. That is, the strategy incrementally explores deeper and deeper nested levels of iteration.

Application

The level-i paths are represented by the numbers of the nodes visited. The level-0 paths are:

1. 1–2–4–5–7–8–9–14–15–17–18
2. 1–2–4–5–7–8–9–14–16–17–18

And the level-1 paths are:

1. 2–3–2
2. 5–6–5
3. 9–10–11–13–9
4. 9–10–12–13–9
5. 17–8

There are no paths higher than level-1. In generating test data to exercise the paths we find that both level-0 paths by themselves are infeasible. To make them feasible we need to incorporate level-1 paths 2 and either 3 (if we want to execute level-0 path 1) or 4 (to execute level-0 path 2). This would lead to test data whereby a character is found in the string and a character is not found in the string. Incorporating the remaining two level-1 paths would require test data to cause iteration of the first *while*-loop (path 1) and to exercise the *repeat*-loop. Combining all these together leads to a set of test requirements that, in this instance, would be covered by the test data generated for branch testing.

It must be noted that level-i paths are not always subsumed by branch testing. Consider the code skeleton example and directed graph shown in Fig. 3.3.

In this case there are four level-i paths as follows:

1. 1–2–4–5–7
2. 1–2–4–6–7
3. 1–3–4–5–7
4. 1–3–4–6–7

Branch testing, on the other hand, would be achieved by covering level-i paths 1 and 4, or 2 and 3.

if (condition – 1) then

(sequence of statements)

else

(sequence of statements)

if (condition – 2) then

(sequence of statements)

else

(sequence of statements)

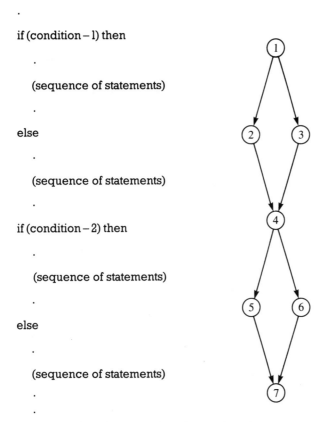

Figure 3.3 Code skeleton example and directed graph.

Strengths and weaknesses

Prather (1983) notes that the *level-i* strategy is readily applicable to both structured and unstructured programs and is a directed strategy. However, finding all the *level-i* paths is computationally expensive and they tend to be large in number. In an excellent comparison of DD-paths, *level-i* paths and linear code sequence and jumps (LCSAJs), Woodward (1984) analysed 116 Fortran programs and found a maximum of 45 287 485 *level-i* (45 287 476 of which were *level-0*) compared with 164 DD-paths and 338 LCSAJs.

References

Further details may be found in Paige (1978), Prather (1983) and Woodward (1984).

3.2.8 Basis path testing

Description

Basis path testing is a way of easily identifying an *upper* bound for the number of paths necessary in order to achieve branch coverage. It is given by the formula for McCabe's Cyclomatic Complexity number (McCabe, 1976) which, given a fully connected (i.e. there is an edge joining the stop node to the start node) directed graph, G, with e edges and n nodes, then the number of linearly independent circuits[1] is given by:

$$V(G) = e - n + 1$$

In our example we have 23 edges and 18 nodes. We need to add an extra edge to join node 18 to node 1 which then gives us a total of 24 edges. So,

$$V(G) = 24 - 18 + 1 = 7$$

We now have to choose seven independent circuits from the graph, say:

1. 1–2–4–5–7–8–9–14–15–17–18–1
2. 1–2–4–5–7–8–9–14–16–17–18–1
3. 2–3–2
4. 5–6–5
5. 9–10–11–13–9
6. 9–10–12–13–9
7. 8–9–15–17–8 ?   8 – 9 – 14 – 15 – 17 – 8
                              8 – 9 – 14 – 16 – 17 – 8

This is known as the *basis set* from which any other path may be built up. For example the path:

$$1–2–3–2–4–5–6–5–6–5–7–8–9–10–11–13–9–14–15–17–18–1$$

is a combination of circuits 1, 3, 4 (twice) and 5. This is justified in terms of vector arithmetic. Each circuit from the basis set may be described by a vector that contains information on the nodes visited by that circuit. So circuits 1, 3, 4 and 5 may be represented by the following vectors:

```
Node:        1  2  3  4  5  6  7  8  9  10 11 12 13 14 15 16 17 18
             -- -- -- -- -- -- -- -- -- -- -- -- -- -- -- -- -- --
Circuit 1:   1  1  0  1  1  0  1  1  1  0  0  0  0  1  1  0  1  1
        3:   0  1  1  0  0  0  0  0  0  0  0  0  0  0  0  0  0  0
        4:   0  0  0  0  1  1  0  0  0  0  0  0  0  0  0  0  0  0
        5:   0  0  0  0  0  0  0  0  1  1  1  0  1  0  0  0  0  0
```

[1] A linearly independent circuit is one that contains at least one new (i.e. previously unvisited) node and starts and finishes on the same node.

So, $1 + 3 + (2 \times 4) + 5$ gives the vector:

$$1 \quad 2 \quad 1 \quad 1 \quad 3 \quad 2 \quad 1 \quad 1 \quad 2 \quad 1 \quad 1 \quad 0 \quad 1 \quad 1 \quad 1 \quad 0 \quad 1 \quad 1$$

which is the same as that which would be derived for our example.

Since the purpose is to ensure branch coverage it is not necessary to show the data generated.

Strengths and weaknesses

The advantages are that the basis set is easily computable and readily applicable to both structured and unstructured programs. However, choosing the basis set is not a simple matter since it is not unique. There are 'obvious' paths that have been left out of the basis (on the theory that they can be formed from the basis set), and different people would choose a different basis set. Furthermore, the number of paths in the basis can greatly exceed the number necessary to achieve branch coverage.

References

For more information see McCabe (1976), Paige and Holthouse (1977), Paige (1978), and Prather (1983).

3.2.9 Path testing

Description

Generate test data to cause execution of all paths in the program. Before continuing it is important to point out the problem with this apparently innocuous statement. A path (in the strictest definition of the term) through a program which makes i iterations of a loop is distinct from a path that makes $i + 1$ iterations—even if the same nodes are visited. So, in our example, we can identify the following paths:

1. 1–2–4–5–6–5–7–8 . . .
2. 1–2–3–2–4–5–6–5–7–8 . . .
3. 1–2–3–2–3–2–4–5–6–5–7–8 . . .
4. etc.

These are considered to be different and distinct paths. It is easy to see that this program is going to have an infinite number of paths. In general, most programs have, at best, a large number of paths and, at worst, an infinite number. A way around this problem is to choose *equivalence classes* of paths. For example, two paths are considered equivalent if they differ only in the number of loop traversals. This will lead to two classes—one with 0 loop traversals—the other with n (where $n > 0$). Other equivalence classes may be chosen, those loops that are iterated just once, for example, but for the purposes of our example we will use the 0 and n case.

Application

If the program is structured then, using a technique described by Paige and Holthouse (1977), it may be characterized by a regular expression of the nodes in the graph where:

·   is the operator applied to sequences,
+   is the operator applied to selections, and
∗   (the Kleene operator) is the operator applied to iterations.

This is best described with a simple example first. Consider the code skeleton and corresponding directed graph shown in Fig. 3.4.

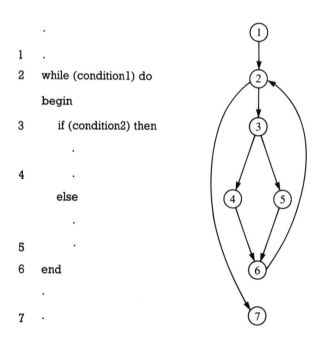

```
       .
1    .
2    while (condition1) do

     begin

3        if (condition2) then

           .

4          .

       else

           .

5          .
6    end

       .

7    .
```

Figure 3.4 Code skeleton and corresponding directed graph.

This can be described by the regular expression:

$$1 \cdot 2 \cdot (3 \cdot (4 + 5) \cdot 6 \cdot 2)^* \cdot 7$$

This may be expanded to give the paths through the program. Before we do this it is necessary to rewrite the expression to generate our equivalence classes of paths (0 iterations and *n* iterations, where *n* is at least 1). This is done by replacing $(x)^*$ with $(x + \circ)$ (where $\circ$ represents *null*). This gives the expression:

$$1 \cdot 2 \cdot ((3 \cdot (4 + 5) \cdot 6 \cdot 2) + \circ) \cdot 7$$

Expanding this gives us the paths through the program. Namely:

1. 1–2–7
2. 1–2–3–4–6–2–7
3. 1–2–3–5–6–2–7

Furthermore, by replacing all values (including the *null*) by 1 and evaluating the expression, the result will be the number of paths through the program. Applying this to the example gives us:

$$1 \cdot 1 \cdot ((1 \cdot (1 + 1) \cdot 1 \cdot 1) + 1) \cdot 1$$

which evaluates to 3.

    This approach needs to be modified slightly to cope with *repeat*-loops. If the previous example involved a *repeat*-loop, it would appear as shown in Fig. 3.5.

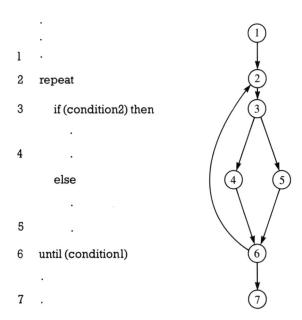

Figure 3.5 Example showing a *repeat*-loop.

Since the *repeat*-loop will be executed at least once, the regular expression has to be written to accommodate this. This may be done as follows:

$$1 \cdot 2 \cdot 3 \cdot (4 + 5) \cdot 6 (\cdot 2 \cdot (3 \cdot (4 + 5) \cdot 6)^* \cdot 7$$

Alternatively, we can introduce the symbol, † to denote a *repeat*-loop whereby $(x)^\dagger$ is expanded to $(x + (x)^2)$. This allows us to write the expression as follows:

$$1 \cdot (2 \cdot 3 \cdot (4 + 5) \cdot 6)^\dagger \cdot 7$$

Either way, substituting all values with 1 gives a total of 6 paths which are:

1. 1–2–3–4–6–7
2. 1–2–3–5–6–7
3. 1–2–3–4–6–2–3–4–6–7
4. 1–2–3–4–6–2–3–5–6–7
5. 1–2–3–5–6–2–3–4–6–7
6. 1–2–3–5–6–2–3–5–6–7

In our example, application of this technique yields the following expression:

$$1 \cdot 2 \cdot (3 \cdot 2)^* \cdot 4 \cdot 5 \cdot (6 \cdot 5)^* \cdot 7 \cdot (8 \cdot 9 \cdot (10 \cdot (11 + 12) \cdot 13 \cdot 9)^*$$
$$\cdot 14 \cdot (15 + 16) \cdot 17)^\dagger \cdot 18$$

Expanding the $(x)^*$ and $(x)^\dagger$ and substituting all values with 1 and evaluating gives us a total of 168 paths! Furthermore, many of these are going to be infeasible. Clearly, generating test data, even for our trivial example, is a time-consuming and tedious task.

Strengths and weaknesses

The weaknesses of path testing should be obvious—there are a lot of paths! However, this is also the strength in that combinations of paths are exercised which other structural coverage methods do not achieve. Again, the conditions within the decisions are not explicitly exercised. In addition, the technique described here for generating paths is not readily applicable to unstructured programs.

References

This subject is also dealt with by Paige and Holthouse (1977) and Prather (1983).

3.2.10 Linear code sequence and jump (LCSAJ)

Description

An LCSAJ is defined by Hennell *et al.* (1984) as follows:

> An LCSAJ start point is the target line of a control flow jump or the first line of the program text. An LCSAJ end point is any line which can be reached from the start point by an unbroken sequence of code and from which a jump can be made. An LCSAJ is characterized by a start line, an end line, and a target line (where it jumps to).

Having identified all the LCSAJs in the program a common aim in testing is to exercise all LCSAJs. This aim can be more precisely expressed using the following test effectiveness ratio:

$$TER_3 = \frac{\text{number of LCSAJs exercised at least once}}{\text{total number of LCSAJs}}$$

TER_3 is an extension of two earlier test effectiveness ratios developed by John Brown of TRW (Brown, 1972). These are:

$$TER_1 = \frac{\text{number of statements exercised at least once}}{\text{total number of executable statements}}$$

$$TER_2 = \frac{\text{number of branches exercised at least once}}{\text{total number of branches}}$$

Higher levels of test effectiveness ratios exist and are expressed in terms of sequences of LCSAJs. A general definition from Woodward *et al.* (1980) is:

$$TER_{n+2} = \frac{x}{y}$$

where, x is the number of distinct subpaths of length n LCSAJs exercised at least once plus the number of distinct complete paths of length less than or equal n LCSAJs exercised at least once, and y is the total number of distinct subpaths of length n LCSAJs plus the total number of distinct complete paths of length less than or equal n LCSAJs.

It is worth looking at a small example (similar to that used in Woodward *et al.* (1980)) to clarify these terms. Consider the following Ada function (with line numbers added for reference). In this example, we can consider execution beginning at line 3. Line 4 contains our first potential jump. Depending on the value of N, either the body of the *for*-loop will be executed or (if $N < 2$) the body will not be executed and control is transferred to line 7. If the body of the loop is executed then there is a jump from line 6 back to line 4 whereupon the condition (based on I and N) is evaluated. When line 7 is reached, the function terminates and so the target jump can be described as 'exit'.

```
1. function FACTORIAL(N:INTEGER) return INTEGER is
2.    RESULT:INTEGER:=1;
3. begin
4.    for I in 2 .. N loop
5.        RESULT := RESULT * I;
6.    end loop;
7.    return RESULT;
8. end FACTORIAL;
```

The LCSAJs for this small example are shown in Table 3.8. The LCSAJs are described in terms of their start line, end line and target line.

Table 3.8 LCSAJs for factorial example

LCSAJ	Start	End	Target
1	3	4	7
2	3	6	4
3	4	6	4
4	4	4	7
5	7	7	exit

Causing the loop not to execute (i.e. $N = 1$) would exercise the first LCSAJ. The remainder would be exercised by causing the loop to iterate twice (i.e. $N = 3$); LCSAJ-2 enters the loop and makes one iteration, LCSAJ-3 makes a second iteration, LCSAJ-4 tests the loop condition and exits the loop and LCSAJ-5 executes the last line of the function. This would achieve the desired goal of $TER_3 = 1$.

Application

The LCSAJs for the example program are shown in Table 3.9. Sometimes the identification of LCSAJs can be quite tricky, especially in cases where the flow of control is not stated explicitly in terms of *GOTO label*. An example of this occurs in identifying the LCSAJs for the *while*-loop. The *end* on line 29 of the program is a syntactic device but for clarity it has been treated as an executable statement—hence its appearance in LCSAJs 11, 13, 14 and 15. It would have been quite possible to have expressed LCSAJ-11 as starting at line 17, ending at line 26 and jumping to line 23. Rewriting LCSAJs 13 and 14 in this way would have made it possible to omit LCSAJ-15 altogether. However, it is hoped that by including LCSAJ-15 the transfer of control is made more explicit and the techniques more understandable.

Table 3.9 LCSAJs for example program

LCSAJ	Start	End	Target
1	6	9	14
2	6	13	9
3	9	13	9
4	9	9	14
5	14	15	17
6	14	16	15
7	15	16	15
8	15	15	17
9	17	23	30
10	17	25	27
11	17	26	29
12	23	25	27
13	27	29	23
14	23	26	29
15	29	29	23
16	23	23	30
17	30	31	34
18	30	30	32
19	32	37	18
20	32	38	exit
21	34	37	18
22	34	38	exit
23	18	23	30
24	18	25	27
25	18	26	29

In order to clarify the production of test data, the test requirements of each of the LCSAJs for the example program are shown in Table 3.10.

To achieve the desired testing goal of $TER_3 = 1$, the two sets of test data shown in Table 3.11 would suffice. The first set of test data would cover LCSAJs 1, 6, 7, 8, 10, 12, 13, 15, 16, 18, 19, 27 and 20. The second set of test data covers LCSAJs 2, 3, 4, 11, 17, 21, 14, 24, 25 and 22.

Strengths and weaknesses

Howden (1976) argues that the detection of a significant number of errors by path testing will depend upon the combination of program branches rather than testing just single branches. Woodward *et al.* (1980) suggest that LCSAJs provide a response to this since branch testing results in, on average, each statement being executed at least twice (Hennell *et al.*, 1983); this figure rises to eight for LCSAJs and it is argued that this increases the fault detection ability. LCSAJs also tend to exercise loops more thoroughly than branch testing (typically three iterations), as well as exercising the case where the loop is not executed.

Table 3.10 LCSAJs and test requirements for example program

LCSAJ	Test requirements
1	First value of x is in range
2	First value of x is out of range
3	Second value of x is out of range
4	Value of x in range—exit loop
5	INFEASIBLE
6	See 8.
7	See 8.
8	Read in a two-component array
9	INFEASIBLE
10	Character does not match first array component
11	Character matches first array component
12	Character does not match after iteration
13	See 12.
14	Character found after iteration
15	Exercise loop
16	Exit loop
17	Character found
18	Character not found
19	Character not found—try again
20	Character not found—exit program
21	Try again
22	Exit program
23	INFEASIBLE
24	Character does not match first array component
25	Character matches first array component

Table 3.11 Test data for LCSAJ coverage

Input				Expected output
x	a	c	*response*	
2	Hw	L		Character L does not occur in the string
			y	
		a		Character a does not occur in the string
			n	
21				Input an integer between 1 and 20
0				Input an integer between 1 and 20
2	tG	t		Character t appears at position 1
			y	
		G		Character G does appear at position 2
			y	
		t		Character t does appears at position 1
			n	

Disadvantages are the difficulties (sometimes) in application to various languages. Luckily, LCSAJs are well supported by tools and so manual analysis of programs does not tend to be necessary. Infeasible paths can also become a problem, especially when higher test effectiveness ratios are attempted (combining more than two LCSAJs).

References

The topic of LCSAJs is dealt with in Woodward *et al.* (1980), which also deals with the practical problems of achieving levels of coverage, Woodward (1984), and Hedley and Hennell (1985) (which takes a thorough look at the problems of infeasible paths within programs). The interested reader should see Hennell *et al.* (1984) for an interesting and thorough informal assessment of the fault-detecting abilities of the various test effectiveness ratios. The tools supporting LCSAJs are described in Hennell *et al.* (1983) and mentioned in several of the other papers.

3.2.11 Data flow testing

Description

The idea behind data flow testing is to generate test data that follow the pattern of data use within a program. The technique of data flow analysis had initially been used to detect anomalies within programs statically (for example, referencing undefined variables) and the idea of using it as a testing technique arose in the 1970s. One of the earliest papers to formalize this approach was that by Laski and Korel (1983). They suggested two testing strategies that were based on exercising pairs of definitions and uses of variables within instructions or blocks. Their approach was extended by Rapps and Weyuker (1985), who classified each occurrence of a variable in a program as being one of the following:

def: definitional
c-use: computational-use
p-use: predicate-use

A definitional occurrence of a variable is one where it appears on, for example, the left-hand side of an assignment statement (i.e. it is given a value). Computational-use is where the variable is used in the evaluation of an expression or an output statement. Predicate-use is where the variable occurs in a predicate (and thereby affects the flow of control of the program). The occurrences of variables in a control-flow graph representation of a program are examined with *p-uses* attributed to the edges and *defs* and *c-uses* attributed to the nodes. A distinction is made between local (i.e. those variables that only occur within one node) and global flows. Rapps and Weyuker identified the following test coverage criteria:

- *all-nodes* (statement coverage)
- *all-edges* (branch coverage)
- *all-defs*
- *all-p-uses*
- *all-c-uses/some-p-uses*
- *all-p-uses/some-c-uses*
- *all-uses*
- *all-du-paths*
- *all-paths*

These coverage criteria may then be ranked according to the partial ordering shown in Fig. 3.6.

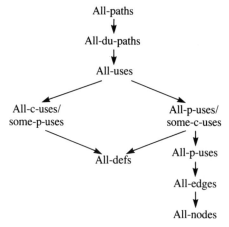

Figure 3.6 Partial ordering of coverage criteria. *Source*: **Rapps and Weyuker (1985)** (© 1985, IEEE).

We will consider the application of the strongest data flow criteria—*all-du-paths*. In this definition, usage includes *c-use* and *p-use* and so no distinction is made between them. The idea is to identify and classify all occurrences of variables in the program and then for each variable generate test data so that all definitions and uses (hereafter known as d–u pairs) are exercised.

As a means of explaining this concept, consider again the Ada function on page 59 (with line numbers added for reference). For this example we shall just concentrate on the variable, *RESULT*. It is defined on line 2, defined and used on line 5, and used on line 7. This allows us to create the list of d–u pairs shown in Table 3.12 with the pairs being expressed in terms of the line numbers on which they appear.

```
1. function FACTORIAL(N:INTEGER) return INTEGER is
2.    RESULT:INTEGER:=1;
3. begin
4.    for I in 2 .. N loop
5.       RESULT := RESULT * I;
6.    end loop;
7.    return RESULT;
8. end FACTORIAL;
```

The 3rd d–u pair might need some explanation. The definition on line 5 takes place on the left-hand side of the assignment statement and this definition is used on the right-hand side, *but after one iteration of the loop.* That is, even though they occur on the same line, the use takes place 'some time' after the variable has been defined. We then need to generate test data to exercise these pairs. Letting *N* have a value of 3 would exercise pairs 1, 3 and 4. Letting *N* have a value of 1 would exercise pair 2.

Table 3.12 d–u pairs for variable RESULT in factorial example

d–u pair	d	u
1	2	5
2	2	7
3	5	5
4	5	7

Application

In our example, the variables we need to deal with are *x*, *i*, *c*, *found*, *response* and the array, *a*.

The d–u pairs for these are shown separately in Tables 3.13, 3.14, 3.15, 3.16, 3.17 and 3.18; again the pairs are identified in terms of the line numbers in the example program.

The test requirements for the variable *x* in Table 3.13 are that a valid value of *x* is supplied at the first input (and then used within the program) and an invalid value of *x* followed by a valid value (which is subsequently used).

With regard to variable *i* in Table 3.14, d–u pair 1 is satisfied by reading at least one value into the array (after which it can be considered to be undefined). Pairs 2 and 3 will be automatically covered. Pair 4 is exercised by unsuccessfully matching the character with the first element in the array. Pair 5, on the other hand, is the result of a successful match with the first

Table 3.13 d–u pairs for variable x in string searching example

d–u pair	d	u
1	8	9
2	8	14
3	8	15
4	8	23
5	12	9
6	12	14
7	12	15
8	12	23

Table 3.14 d–u pairs for variable i in string searching example

d–u pair	d	u
1	15	16
2	22	23
3	22	25
4	22	28
5	22	31
6	28	23
7	28	25
8	28	28
9	28	31

element in the array. Pairs 6 to 9 are exercised by a further unsuccessful match followed by a successful match.

The d–u pairs for variable c are shown in Table 3.15. These are satisfied by successfully finding character c in the array and not finding c in the array. A similar requirement exists for the variable *found* whose d–u pairs are shown in Table 3.16.

Table 3.15 d–u pairs for variable c in string searching example

d–u pair	d	u
1	20	25
2	20	31
3	20	33

Table 3.16 d–u pairs for variable
found **in string searching example**

d–u pair	d	u
1	21	23
2	21	30
3	26	23
4	26	30

The d–u pair for *response* is shown in Table 3.17 and this is easily exercised by supplying a value of 'y' for *response*.

Table 3.17 d–u pairs for variable
response **in string searching example**

d–u pair	d	u
1	36	37

The array *a* poses a problem for data flow testing since we are frequently unable to determine which element in the array is being used—that is, it is not uniquely identifiable. For example, if an array is subscripted by two variables *j* and *k* whose values dynamically change according to the execution of the program then it is frequently impossible to determine what values *j* and *k* hold. The solution to this is to treat the entire array as one variable. The d–u pair for *a* is shown in Table 3.18 and this is simply exercised by the normal execution of the program.

Table 3.18 d–u pairs for variable *a* in
string searching example

d–u pair	d	u
1	16	25

Table 3.19 shows the entire set of test data needed to satisfy the requirements of data flow testing.

Strengths and weaknesses

It is argued that one of the advantages of data flow testing is that it generates test data according to the way that data are manipulated within the program

Table 3.19 Test data for data flow testing

Input				Expected output
x	a	c	response	
1	D	D	n	Character D appears at position 1
21 3	XYZ	Z a	y n	Input an integer between 1 and 20 Character Z appears at position 3 Character a does not occur in the string

rather than following 'artificial' control constructs. The difficulties are in the application in the presence of dynamically bound data such as pointers. Weyuker (1988b) performed an empirical study of data flow testing. Although the theoretical limit of the number of test cases is exponential (2^d, where d is the number of two-way decisions in the program), in practice only small numbers (relative to the size of the program) of test cases are needed. This result is corroborated by Bieman and Schultz (1989) who studied a natural language text analysis system totalling 143 subroutines (with an average length of 52 lines and a maximum of 367). They found that 115 (80 per cent) of the subroutines could be tested with 10 or fewer complete paths, and 91 per cent could be met with 25 or fewer complete paths. Only four required more than 100 paths, one needed 10 000 and another (consisting of a sequence of 32 if-statements) went exponential with 2^{32} paths.

References

The definitive references for data flow testing are Laski and Korel (1983), Ntafos (1984) and Rapps and Weyuker (1985). A good theoretical comparison of data flow testing strategies is to be found in Clarke *et al.* (1985).

The static application of data flow analysis (for example, to detect anomalies such as undefined variables without executing the program) is discussed in Osterweil (1977), Jachner and Agarwal (1984) and Forman (1984).

3.2.12 Domain testing

Description

The basic idea of domain testing is to consider the path predicates in the program and see which values from the input space (the domain) will cause the path to be executed. That is, we chop up the domain into a number of regions and all the data chosen from one region will cause the same path to be executed. The testing strategy then involves examining each of the borders of each region in detail and selecting test data near the border. The whole idea is to try to detect 'border shifts'—that is, incorrect predicates in the program. The strategy can be seen as a kind of formalized *boundary value analysis*.

Having described the strategy very informally, it is now time to treat it with a little more rigour. A border is defined by the path predicates in the program and may be either a *closed* border (where the predicates are written in terms of the relational operators $<=, =, >=$) or an *open* border (involving the remaining relational operators). Only closed borders need be tested since the open border of a path domain is the closed border of the adjacent domain. The border under test is known as the *given* border. When the given border differs from the correct border then a *domain shift* is said to have occurred. Putting this in simple terms, the given border might have been bounded by the predicate:

.

```
if X <= 4 then
```

.

.

whereas the correct border should have been:

.

```
if X <= 5 then
```

.

.

The goal of the domain testing strategy is to detect shifts such as these.

The creation of test data for the given boundary seeks to create two types of boundary test points:

ON: these are on the given border and within the domain under test.
OFF: these are outside the given border and within some adjacent domain.

If the program produces correct results for all the ON and OFF test points then the given border can be considered to be equal to (or at least very close to—depending on the distance of the OFF test points from the border) the correct border. Figure 3.7 illustrates the terminology associated with domain testing.

For a simple two-dimensional domain, White and Cohen (1980) suggest selecting two ON test points and one OFF test point. The ON test points should be placed as close as possible to the ends of the given border. This closeness depends on whether the border is bounded by a closed border (in which case the test point is at the very end of the given border) or by an open

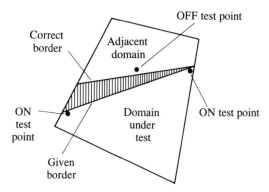

Figure 3.7 Illustration of domain testing terminology. *Source*: Clarke and Richardson (1982) (© 1982, IEEE).

border (in which case the test point is as close as possible to the end of the given border). The OFF test point is strictly between the two ON test points on the open side of the given border and should lie a small distance from it. In addition, the OFF test point should satisfy all the inequalities that define the domain under test except the one corresponding to the given border—this is to ensure that we concentrate on testing just one border at a time. As an extension to this strategy and to limit the error tolerance of the technique, Clarke *et al.* (1982) suggest selecting two OFF test points at the ends of the given border.

Application

Domain testing is one of the techniques that is not readily applicable to our example (the reasons for this are discussed in the section on strengths and weaknesses). We shall therefore demonstrate its application to the following rather abstract program (with the predicates labelled P1, P2 and P3 for reference) written in pseudocode:

```
begin program domaintest
    variables: a,b,x,y: real;
    read(x,y)
if y <= 5.0 then    (P1)
    a := x - y - 2
else
    a := x + y - 2;
if a < -3.0 then    (P2)
    b := a + x + 2y + 3;
else
    b := a - 7y + 3;
if b <= 7.0 then    (P3)
    print(x);
```

```
else
    print(y);
end program
```

Figure 3.8 shows the domains created from the 'domaintest' program.

The next step is to select the ON and OFF test points. The first ON test point can be chosen at the intersection between the predicates P1 and P2. This gives us a value of $y = 5.0$ and $x = 4.0$. The second ON test point is defined by the intersection of predicates P2 and P3 but is further constrained to lie on the 'open' side of P3. Suitable data would be $x = 1.67$ and $y = 2.67$. The OFF test point (we shall just choose one for the purposes of explanation) is chosen at the midpoint of the given boundary at, say $x = 2.5, y = 3.5$. These points are illustrated in Fig. 3.8. One way of identifying these domains is by *symbolic execution* which is discussed in Sec. 3.2.13 on partition analysis.

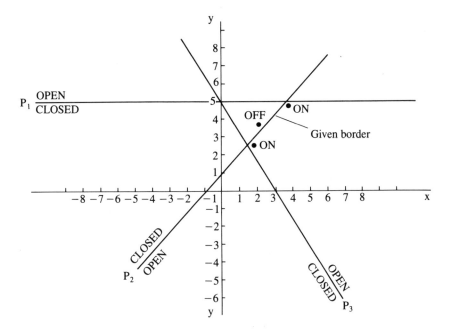

Figure 3.8 Domains created by domaintest program with ON and OFF test points.

Strengths and weaknesses

The advantage of domain testing is that it gives explicit guidance in the selection of data to test predicate boundaries. Furthermore, the selection of two OFF test points means that the size of the error (the possible boundary shift) can be constrained and quantified.

There are, however, a number of weaknesses or, more correctly, restrictions imposed on the method. In the initial definition of the methods by White and Cohen (1980), the input space was deemed to be continuous and the predicate interpretations simple linear inequalities. White and Cohen provide the following succinct explanation of linear and non-linear predicates. A predicate is said to be linear in variables $V_1, V_2 \ldots V_n$ if it is of the form $A_1 V_1 + A_2 V_2 + \ldots + A_n V_n$ ROP K where K and A_i are constants and ROP is one of the relational operators $<, >, =, \neq, \geq, \leq$. A compound predicate is linear when each of its component linear predicates are linear.

For example, if x, y and z are variables within a program then $3x + 234y - z \leq 5$ is a linear predicate in terms of the variables x, y and z. $2x^4 - y + z^2 = 12$ is not linear.

A path through a program can be described as a conjunction of predicates in terms of the program's input variables. If this conjunction of predicates is linear then a solution to this may be found, and (if the path is feasible) the path executed (although finding a solution may involve the use of heuristic search algorithms).

A further restriction on the method was that coincidental correctness was assumed not to occur. Coincidental correctness occurs when incorrect code produces the correct values for the chosen test data. A simple illustration of this is given below:

```
Correct Code          Incorrect Code
-----------           --------------
      .                     .
      .                     .
      .                     .
x := y * y            x := y + y
      .                     .
      .                     .
      .                     .
```

In this example a portion of a program has been incorrectly coded to add y to itself and assign the result to x rather than to square it. This incorrect code will produce coincidentally correct results if y is given values 0 or 2. White (1985) gives some interesting examples of coincidental correctness as well as an overview of the subject of domain testing.

Clarke *et al.* (1982) have relaxed some of these restrictions so that discrete domains can be handled and, rather than assuming that coincidental correctness does not occur, instead assume that the domains adjacent to the given one perform recognizably different computations. Nevertheless, the application of the technique to a problem such as ours involving loops and character data is beyond the current technology.

References

The technique was initially defined by White and Cohen (1980) and has been thoroughly analysed by Clarke and Richardson (1983a, 1983b; Richardson and Clarke, 1985b), who also contributed to the best overview of the method (Clarke *et al.* 1982).

3.2.13 Partition analysis

Description

Partition analysis is closely related to the idea of domain testing. The major difference is that it takes into account the specification as well as the program. As a consequence it is one of the few techniques to integrate formally functional and structural (or black-box and white-box) testing techniques.

Like domain testing the technique relies on performing a *symbolic execution* of the specification and the program. Symbolic execution or symbolic evaluation is performed by letting input variables take on symbolic names and then executing the program by hand. The result will be an equation in terms of the input variables which, if satisfied, will cause the symbolically executed path to be executed. A small example might help to illustrate the idea. Consider the program segment below:

```
read(x)
y := x * x;
if y < 7 then
    .
    .
    .
else
    .
    .
    .
```

To execute it symbolically we let x have the value x (this may seem a little strange but we have to give x a symbolic name and what better one than its own name!). The next step in the program results in y having a symbolic value of x * x. We then encounter the *if*-statement and, for the *true* outcome to be taken, then the inequality x * x < 7 must hold (i.e. we refer to the symbolic value of y). The technique is difficult to apply in the presence of such features as arrays and pointers. Loops can also present a problem but may be circumvented in a similar way to path testing by creating two paths—one that executes the loop and one that does not (the number of loop executions is sometimes limited to one or two, after which a 'picture' of the computation should start to appear). For more information on the topic see Richardson and Clarke (1985b), for example.

In carrying out partition analysis the path domains and path computations are calculated for the specification and the implementation. A path domain describes the conditions that must hold for input data to be selected within that domain. All data within one domain are treated identically. A path computation describes the computations carried out on any data falling within that domain. The next step is to create a procedure partition. This is done by effectively overlaying the specification and implementation partitions. Sometimes there will be a one-to-one match between a specification partition and an implementation partition (which means that all data within a partition are treated identically by both the specification and the implementation). Sometimes there will be no overlap between a specification and implementation partition—this is a problem since it means that no data exist to execute the computation specified. The third alternative is that there will be overlaps between specification and implementation domains, which means there is a mismatch between the two. This may occur, for example, when one set of data from the specification has been treated in different ways by the implementation.

The partition analysis strategy results in formal (i.e. symbolic) representations of the specification and implementation. This representation is exploited by carrying out a formal verification to try and show consistency between the computation carried out by the specification and that carried out by the corresponding path or paths. This, however, is beyond the scope of this book.

The actual testing done from partition analysis is relatively straightforward and employs techniques aimed at revealing *computation errors* (such as getting computations to evaluate to zero, letting terms take on values such as $-1, 0$ *or* 1, and using extremal data) and *domain errors* (typically, domain testing is used for this). The argument for this is that the creation of a procedure partition has formed an object which is a rich description of the relationship between the implementation and the specification. The creation of this partition procedure alone has done a lot of the work in choosing the test data.

Application

Like domain testing, application to our original example is not ideal for describing partition analysis. To demonstrate the technique, consider first of all this simple program (referred to as 'Grader'):

```
A course taught at a university has two components:
an exam and a piece of coursework.
To pass the course with grade C a student must score
at least 50% in the exam and 50% in the coursework.
They pass the course with grade B if they score at
least 60% in the exam and 50% in the coursework.
If, in addition to this the average of the exam and
coursework is at least 70% then they are awarded a
grade A.
```

```
program Grader(Input, Output);
var
  Exam, Course, Average: real;
begin
  Write('Input exam mark: ');
  ReadLn(Exam);
  Write('Input course mark: ');
  ReadLn(Course);
  if (Exam < 0 ) or (Exam > 100) or
    (Course < 0 ) or (Course > 100) then
    WriteLn('Marks out of range - program terminating')
  else
      if (Exam < 50) or (Course < 50) then
        WriteLn('Fail')
      else if (Exam < 60) then
            WriteLn('Pass - Grade C')
          else
            if (Exam + Course)/2 >= 70 then
            begin
              Average := (Exam + Course)/2;
    WriteLn('Pass - Grade A with an average mark of ',
Average:5:2)
            end;)
            else
    WriteLn('Pass - Grade B')
end.
```

Performing a symbolic evaluation of the specification we end up with the following domains (D) and associated computations (C) shown below. The 'S' refers to specification ('P' is for program) and the subscript is just an arbitrary identifier of the partition. Note that the computations are very simple consisting, for the most part, of output.

$D[S_1]$ (Exam < 50) or (Course < 50)
$C[S_1]$ Output—'Fail'
$D[S_2]$ (Exam $\geq$ 50) and (Exam < 60) and (Course $\geq$ 50)
$C[S_2]$ Output—'Pass – Grade C'
$D[S_3]$ (Exam $\geq$ 60) and (Course $\geq$ 50) and ((Exam + Course) $\div$ 2 < 70)
$C[S_3]$ Output—'Pass – Grade B'
$D[S_4]$ (Exam $\geq$ 60) and (Course $\geq$ 50) and ((Exam + Course) $\div$ 2 $\geq$ 70)
$C[S_4]$ Output—'Pass – Grade A'

Figure 3.9 shows the domains created from this specification.

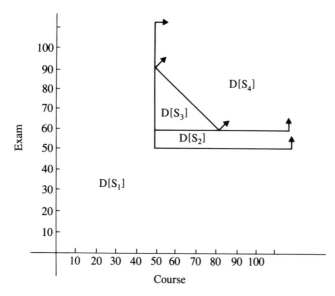

Figure 3.9 Domains created by symbolic evaluation of grader program specification.

Performing a similar process on the program reveals the following partitions and computations.

$D[P_1]$ (Exam < 0) or (Course < 0) or (Exam > 100) or (Course > 100)
$C[P_1]$ Output—'Marks out of range – program terminating'
$D[P_2]$ $\neg D[P_1]$ and ((Exam < 50) or (Course < 50))
$C[P_2]$ Output—'Fail'
$D[P_3]$ $\neq D[P_1]$ and ((Exam $\geq$ 50) and (Exam < 60) and (Course $\geq$ 50))
$C[P_3]$ Output—'Pass – Grade C'
$D[P_4]$ $\neg D[P_1]$ and ((Exam $\geq$ 60) and (Course $\geq$ 50) and ((Exam + Course) $\div$ 2 < 70))
$C[P_4]$ Output—'Pass – Grade B'
$D[P_5]$ $\neg D[P_1]$ and ((Exam $\geq$ 60) and (Course $\geq$ 50) and ((Exam + Course) $\div$ 2 $\geq$ 70))
$C[P_5]$ Average = (Exam + Class) $\div$ 2 and Output—'Pass – Grade A with an average mark of' Average

Figure 3.10 shows the domains created from this program.

The next step is to create the *procedure partition*. This is done by taking the domains created by symbolic evaluation of the specification (individually known as sub-specification domains) and those created by symbolic evaluation of the implementation (individually known as path domains). The procedure subdomain is then defined as the non-empty intersection of the sub-specification domain ($D[S_i]$) and the path domain ($D[P_j]$), and is denoted by D_{ij}. For each procedure subdomain created from

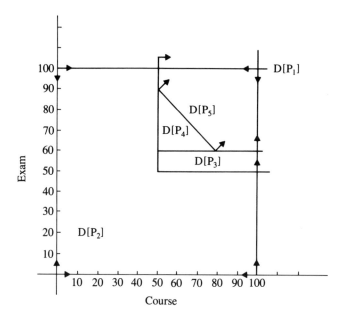

Figure 3.10 Domains created by symbolic evaluation of grader program implementation.

a non-empty intersection there will be two computations—one defined by the sub-specification and one defined by the path. If these computations should turn out to be different, then the computation (C_{ij}) is the symbolic difference between the sub-specification computation $(C[S_i])$ and the path computation $(C[P_j])$. This is denoted using the symbolic evaluation difference operator as $C_{ij} = C[S_i] \ominus C[P_j]$. This occurs in our example when the average is calculated and output if the highest grade is achieved. This was not specified and appears as an 'unrequested extra' in the program.

Sometimes the specification and implementation domains are non-compatible. This may occur when there are input data in a sub-specification domain which are not treated by any of the path domains (denoted by D_{i0}) or conversely there are some input data handled by a path domain which are not dealt with by any of the sub-specification domains (denoted by D_{0j}). An obvious example of the latter is where the implementation might trap some out-of-range data, whereas the specification only defines what is to be done with data that fall in range; this is the case with our example.

The procedure partition of 'Grader' is:

D_{01} (Exam < 0) or (Course < 0) or (Exam > 100) or (Course > 100)
C_{01} Output—'Marks out of range – program terminating'
D_{12} ¬D_{01} and ((Exam < 50) or (Course < 50))

C_{12} Output—'Fail'

D_{23} $\neg D_{01}$ and ((Exam $\geq$ 50) and (Exam $<$ 60) and (Course $\geq$ 50))

C_{23} Output—'Pass – Grade C'

D_{34} $\neg D_{01}$ and ((Exam $\geq$ 60) and (Course $\geq$ 50) and ((Exam + Course) $\div$ 2 $<$ 70))

C_{34} Output—'Pass – Grade B'

D_{45} $\neg D_{01}$ and ((Exam $\geq$ 60) and (Course $\geq$ 50) and ((Exam + Course) $\div$ 2 $\geq$ 70))

C_{45} Output—'Pass – Grade A' $\ominus$ Average = (Exam + Class) $\div$ 2 and Output—'Pass – Grade A with an average mark of' Average

Figure 3.11 shows the procedure partition for this program.

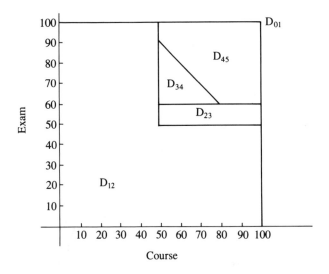

Figure 3.11 Procedure partition for grader program.

The next step is to create the test data from this procedure partition. Most of the tests are based on the domain boundaries and concentrate on the points on either side of these boundaries. There is one computation to test— the calculation of *average*. To test this will require allocating minimum and maximum values for the variables that are allowable within the constraints of the domain.

Table 3.20 shows the set of test data (assuming two decimal places of precision) needed to satisfy the requirements of partition analysis testing. The test data are grouped by procedure partition to show how they were derived.

Table 3.20 Test data for partition analysis testing

Procedure partition	Input		Expected output
	Exam	Course	
D_{01}	0.0	0.0	Fail
	0.0	100.0	Fail
	100.0	0.0	Fail
	100.0	100.0	Grade A – Average = 100
	50.0	–0.01	Out of range
	50.0	100.01	Out of range
	–0.01	50.0	Out of range
	100.01	50.0	Out of range
D_{12}	50.0	100.0	Grade C
	100.0	50.0	Grade A – Average = 75.0
	49.99	49.99	Fail
D_{23}	50.0	50.0	Grade C
	50.0	100.0	Grade C
	49.99	75.0	Fail
D_{34}	60.0	50.0	Grade B
	60.0	100.0	Grade A – Average = 80.0
	59.99	75.0	Grade C
D_{45}	90.0	50.0	Grade A – Average = 70.0
	60.0	80.0	Grade A – Average = 70.0
	64.99	74.99	Grade B
C_{45}	100.0	100.0	Grade A – Average = 100.0
	70.0	70.0	Grade A – Average = 70.0

Strengths and weaknesses

Richardson and Clarke (1985a) describe a limited evaluation carried out as part of their research into the technique. They took a number of small programs and procedures from the literature and wrote the specifications (since they were unavailable). They use *mutation analysis* and lists of common faults to systematically seed faults into the program. In one study, out of 25 faults, eight were found during the process of symbolic evaluation, two by partition analysis testing, and the remainder were found by both partition analysis verification and testing (i.e. either technique would have exposed the fault). Another evaluation created 363 mutant programs containing domain and computation errors, of which 295 were found and the remainder deemed to be equivalent to the original program (see Secs 3.2.18 and 3.2.19 on mutation testing for more details of the terminology used here). None of the programs involved missing path faults but the feeling is that the method would be reasonably effective at finding these. In short, the combination of symbolic evaluation and testing seems to be a powerful one although the method has practical limitations when, for example, loop representations become too complex to handle.

References

The main references for partition analysis are the works of Richardson and Clarke (1981, 1985a). The interested reader might also like to consider the related work on revealing subdomains by Weyuker and Ostrand (1980).

3.2.14 Equivalence partitioning

Description

Equivalence partitioning is a technique that is based on the specification and does not draw on the details of the program in any way. The basis of the idea is to divide up the input domain into *equivalence partitions* or *classes* of data which, according to the specification, are treated identically. The basis of the technique is that any datum chosen from an equivalence class is as valid as any other since it should be processed in a similar fashion. In short, the technique is based upon reducing the input domain to a manageable and testable size. In addition to this, the output domain should also be treated in the same way and 'reverse engineered' to be expressed in terms of the input domain. To assist in the identification of partitions, Myers (1979) suggests looking in the specification for terms such as 'range' and 'set' and other similar words which indicate that data are processed identically. Equivalence classes must not overlap, so any such cases must be reduced, if possible, to separate and distinct classes.

Having identified the equivalence partitions, one datum is chosen from each partition. In addition to this, invalid data may also be chosen (i.e. data that lie outside the class and are not explicitly processed by any other class; this is frequently useful when testing 'validation' type programs).

Application

Considering our original example (the string searching program) there are, according to the specification, basically four inputs:

- A positive integer
- A string of characters
- A character to be searched for
- The option to search for more characters

It is stated that the positive integer has to be in the range 1 to 20, so three equivalence partitions are immediately apparent: one consisting of integers in the stated range and the other two consisting of integers either side of this range. The integer determines the length of the character string to be input.

Nothing is said about different characters or different lengths of string being treated in dissimilar fashions, so no further equivalence partitions can be identified at this point. The option to search for more characters is just a binary choice that forms two partitions—one for 'yes' and the other for 'no'.

The next stage is to consider the output domain which consists of two responses:

- The position at which the character was found in the string.
- A message stating that it was not found.

This information can now be used to further subdivide our input domain into two partitions: one containing characters that are found in the string and the other containing characters that are absent from the string.

Putting all this information together we end up with the set of test data shown in Table 3.21. It must be stated that the choice of data within the partitions (a string of length 3, the characters 'abc' and so on) is quite arbitrary since all data are assumed to be equally valid.

Table 3.21 Test data for equivalence partitioning

Input				Expected output
x	a	c	*response*	
34				Input an integer between 1 and 20
0				Input an integer between 1 and 20
3	abc	c		Character c appears at position 3
			y	
		k		Character k does not occur in the string
			n	

Strengths and weaknesses

The strength of equivalence partitioning is that it does help to reduce the apparent size of the input domain and focuses on creating test cases based purely on the specification. The method is particularly well suited to data processing-type applications where the input variables may be easily identified and take on distinct values. It is less easily applicable in the complementary situation where the input domain is simple, yet the processing is complex. A further possible problem is that, although the specification may suggest that a group of data is processed identically, this may not in fact be the case. This serves to reinforce the argument that functional (black-box or specification-based) testing techniques and structural (white-box or code-based) testing techniques should be used in conjunction. A further drawback is that the technique provides very little guidance for the creation of test data or assistance in finding combinations of test data.

References

The main reference for this technique is Myers (1979).

3.2.15 Boundary value analysis

Description

Boundary value analysis is a technique that is used in conjunction with equivalence partitioning in that it focuses on a fruitful source of faults—the boundaries of an equivalence partition (or class). The technique relies on having created the equivalence partition and then derives test data by examining the edges of the partition. Figure 3.12 illustrates this idea.

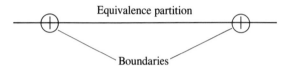

Figure 3.12 Test data selection using boundary value analysis.

Application

Having identified the equivalence partitions (see Sec. 3.2.14) it is a relatively straightforward matter to identify the boundaries. So, for our example, integer values of 0, 1, 20 and 21 are obvious choices, as well as finding the character in the first position and the last position in the string. Myers (1979) would also advocate such things as using strings composed of all the same character, although this involves perhaps a more inventive interpretation of the method. The set of test data shown in Table 3.22 shows that created using this technique.

Strengths and weaknesses

The strengths and weaknesses of boundary value analysis are similar to those of equivalence partitioning. An additional strength is that it does provide more guidance in the creation of test data and these test data do tend to be focused on an area where faults tend to be found. The technique is similar to (but less powerful than) partition analysis.

References

The main reference for this technique is Myers (1979).

Table 3.22 Test data for boundary value analysis

Input				Expected output
x	a	c	response	
21				Input an integer between 1 and 20
0				Input an integer between 1 and 20
1	a	a		Character a appears at position 1
			y	
		X		Character X does not occur in the string
			n	
20	abcdefghijklmnopqrst	a		Character a appears at position 1
			y	
		t		Character t appears at position 20
			n	

3.2.16 Cause–effect graphing

Description

Cause–effect graphing is a functional or specification-based technique which aims to create 'interesting' combinations of test data. The specification is analysed, and causes (inputs, stimuli, or anything that is going to elicit a response from the system under test) and effects (outputs, changes in the system state or any observable response) are identified. The causes and effects have to be stated in a way such that they may either be true or false. For example, if a section of a specification stated, 'If the record is present on the master file then a report line is written', then the cause would have to be expressed as, 'Record present on master file', and the effect as, 'Report line written'. This is necessary because the causes and effects are going to be combined in a Boolean graph that describes the relationships between them.

Having identified the causes and effects, they are each allocated an arbitrary unique number for reference. The next step is to create the Boolean graph that shows the logical relationships linking the causes and effects.

Graphs may be combined using the operators:

$$AND \quad \wedge$$
$$NAND \quad \not\wedge$$
$$NOT \quad \sim$$
$$OR \quad \vee$$
$$NOR \quad \not\vee$$

To illustrate these, a number of example graphs are shown in Fig. 3.13. For the purposes of this illustration it is immaterial what the actual causes and effects are.

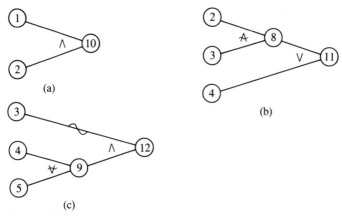

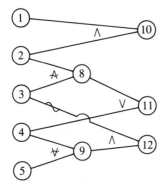

Figure 3.13 Construction of an example cause–effect graph.

Effect 10 occurs (Fig. 3.13a) if both causes 1 and 2 are present. Effect 11 occurs (Fig. 3.13b) if causes 2 and 3 are not both present or cause 4 is present. Effect 12 occurs (Fig. 3.13c) if neither causes 4 or 5 are present and cause 3 is absent. The complete subgraph is shown in Fig. 3.14.

Figure 3.14 Completed cause–effect subgraph.

In addition, *environmental constraints* might occur and further limit the possible combinations of causes and effects in the graph. For example, it may not be possible to have two particular causes present at the same time, or one effect might override any other effect. The possible environmental constraints are:

I	At least one (inclusive)
E	At most one (exclusive)
O	One and only one
R	Requires
M	Masks

Further constraints on this example are that cause 1 is always present, one and only one of causes 2 and 5 may occur, cause 5 also requires cause 6, and effect 12 masks effect 10. The complete graph is as shown in Fig. 3.15.

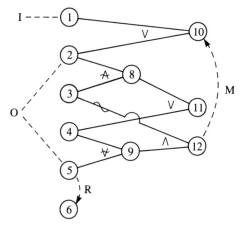

Figure 3.15 Example cause–effect graph showing environmental constraints.

The next step is to systematically work through the graph and convert it into a decision table. The decision table shows the effects occurring for every possible combination of causes. Of course, given n causes, this would lead to a decision table with 2^n entries. In practice, the presence of environmental constraints tend to reduce the number of entries. In the decision table, a '1' indicates that a cause or effect is present and a '0' that it is absent. It is also permissible to indicate that they may be irrelevant by a '-'. The decision table for this abstract example is shown in Fig. 3.16.

```
 1 |  1  1  1  1  1  1  1  1
 2 |  1  0  0  0  1  1  1  1
 3 |  0  1  0  1  1  0  1  0
 4 |  0  0  1  1  0  1  1  0
 5 |  0  1  1  1  0  0  0  1
 6 |  0  1  1  1  0  0  0  1
   ------------------------
10 |  1  0  0  0  1  1  1  0
11 |  1  1  1  1  0  1  1  1
12 |  1  0  0  0  0  0  0  0
```

Figure 3.16 Decision table for abstract example.

The final step is to convert each column into a test case by referring back to the original list of causes and effect and invoking those that are true and suppressing those that are false. The expected output is defined in a similar way.

Application

Applying this to our string searching example we can identify the causes:

1. Positive integer in range 1–20
2. Character to be searched for is in string
3. Search for another character

and effects:

20. Integer out of range
21. Position of character in string reported
22. Character not found
23. Program terminates

The cause–effect graph is shown in Fig. 3.17 and the associated decision table in Fig. 3.18. This would translate into the four test cases shown in Table 3.23.

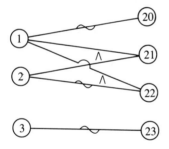

Figure 3.17 Cause–effect graph for string searching example.

```
 1 |  0  1  1  -
 2 |  -  1  0  -
 3 |  -  1  1  0
-----------
20 |  1  0  0  0
21 |  0  1  0  0
22 |  0  0  1  0
23 |  0  0  0  1
```

Figure 3.18 Decision table for string searching example.

Table 3.23 Test data for cause–effect graphing

Input				Expected output
x	a	c	response	
23 3	abc	c k	 y n	Input an integer between 1 and 20 Character c appears at position 3 Character k does not occur in the string

As a further, and perhaps more appropriate, illustration of the method we will also apply it to the exam grading example, 'Grader'. We can identify the following causes:

1. Exam < 50
2. Course < 50
3. Exam ≥ 50 and < 60
4. Exam ≥ 60
5. (Exam + Course)÷2 ≥ 70

and effects:

20. Fail
21. Pass – Grade A
23. Pass – Grade B
24. Pass – Grade C

The cause–effect graph is shown in Fig. 3.19 and the associated decision table in Fig. 3.20. This would translate into the eight test cases shown in shown in Table 3.24.

Table 3.24 Test data for cause–effect graphing

Test case	Input		Expected output
	Exam	Course	
1	25.0	60.0	Fail
2	25.0	25.0	Fail
3	55.0	25.0	Fail
4	65.0	25.0	Fail
5	100.0	45.0	Fail
6	55.0	52.0	Grade C
7	67.0	56.0	Grade B
8	80.0	80.0	Grade A

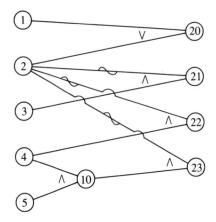

Figure 3.19 Cause–effect graph for exam grading example.

```
 1 |  1 1 0 0 0 0 0 0
 2 |  0 1 1 1 1 1 0 0 0
 3 |  0 0 1 0 0 1 0 0
 4 |  0 0 0 1 1 0 1 1
 5 |  0 0 0 0 1 0 0 1
   -------------------
20 |  1 1 1 1 1 0 0 0
21 |  0 0 0 0 0 1 0 0
22 |  0 0 0 0 0 0 1 0
23 |  0 0 0 0 0 0 0 1
```

Figure 3.20 Decision table for exam grading example.

Strengths and weaknesses

The strength of cause–effect graphing is that it does exercise combinations of test data that might not otherwise have been tried. A further strength of the method is that the expected results are produced as part of the test creation process. The major drawback with the method is creating the Boolean graph—given a large number of causes and effects, this can very quickly become highly complex. A possible solution to this is the attempt to identify independent sub-problems and develop separate cause–effect graphs for these. Like other functional testing methods, the effectiveness of cause–effect graphing is dependent on the quality of the specification for identifying the causes and effects. A very detailed specification, for example, will probably lead to a large number of causes and effects whereas a more abstract and general specification will lead to fewer causes and effects and consequently less effective test cases.

References

The main reference for this technique is Elmendorf (1973), but Myers (1979) also gives it a very thorough treatment.

3.2.17 Category–partition testing

Description

Category–partition testing (Ostrand and Balcer, 1988) is related in many ways to equivalence partitioning, boundary value analysis and cause–effect graphing, as well as to domain testing and partition analysis. It seeks to generate test cases that 'cover' the function and maximize the number of faults found. This is done by exercising all combinations of distinct groups of values of input parameters. In summary, the method identifies the parameters of each 'function' and, for each parameter, identifies distinct characteristics termed 'categories'. The categories are further subdivided into 'choices' in the same way as equivalence partitioning is applied. The constraints operating between choices are then identified (for example, one choice may require that another is absent, or has a particular value). Finally, test frames are generated which consist of the allowable combinations of choices in the categories. These test frames are then converted into actual test data.

The method is more precisely described by the following steps:

1. Decompose the functional specification into units that can be tested independently.
2. Identify parameters and environment conditions (e.g. the state of the system at the time of execution) that affect the function's behaviour.
3. Find categories (major properties or characteristics) of information that characterize each parameter and environment condition.
4. Partition each category into choices that include all the different kinds of values that are possible for the category. A choice is a set of similar values and defines the partition class from which representative elements will be taken to build test cases.
5. Write the formal test specification. This consists of a list of categories and a list of choices within each category.
6. Create test frames by choosing a set of choices from the test specification (each category contributes zero or one choice).
7. Create test cases by choosing a single element for each choice in the test frame.

The concept of a category is deserving of a little more explanation. Ostrand and Balcer give the example of a function that is to take as input a variable length array of any type and return the sorted array (according to some criterion) and the maximum and minimum values. They identify the categories as being:

- The array's size
- Type of elements
- Maximum element value
- Minimum element value
- Positions in the array of the maximum and minimum element values

Choices are then made for each category. Choices are based on the specification, the experience of the tester, knowledge of likely error situations, and even the internal structure of the code. So, typical choices for the above would include an array of size 0, of size 1 and of size 2 to n (where n is the maximum size), and an attempt at $n + 1$. The maximum value would be in the first, middle and last places in the array, and so on.

The above set of steps will tend to yield a large number of test cases for any reasonably sized application, and so a way has been defined to cut down on the number of test cases generated. This is done by adding more information to the choices. The choices may be annotated with constraints as a way of limiting the number of test cases. These constraints may consist of properties or attributes, and selectors based on properties. The choices will only be combined into the test frame if the selector is true. For example, given the following example with two categories and two choices within each category:

```
Category A
  ChoiceA1
  ChoiceA2
Category B
  ChoiceB1
  ChoiceB2
```

This would normally yield four test frames (all combinations of choices). But by annotating these with properties, and defining selectors on those properties we can reduce the number of frames. For example:

```
Category A
  ChoiceA1 [property X]
  ChoiceA2
Category B
  ChoiceB1
  ChoiceB2 [if X]
```

We have given ChoiceA1 some property called X and ChoiceB2 is a selector on this property. This means that ChoiceA2 and ChoiceB2 would not be combined into a test frame since ChoiceA2 does not have property X associated with it.

Other annotations available are [error] (designed to test an error state and not to be combined with any other choices) and [single] (for special, or redundant choices which again do not have to be combined with any others).

Application

Using our string searching example we are able to work through the steps of the method as follows:

1. *Decompose the functional specification*—The specification is small enough as it is and does not require further decomposition.
2. *Identify parameters and environment conditions*—There are three parameters, the integer x, the string a and the character c.
3. *Find categories*—For x the categories are that it is in range (1–20) or out of range. For a the categories are that it is of minimal, maximal and intermediate length. Finally, categories for c are that it should appear at the beginning, middle and end of the string, or not appear in the string.
4. *Partition each category into choices*—Choices for the integer x being out of range could include the values 0 and 21 (we could also add in negative integers if we wished), and in range values are 1, 2–19, and 20. Choices for the length of the string a are 1, 2–19, and 20 (since this is dependent on the integer x. Choices for the character c is that it occupies the first, middle and last positions in the string, or does not occur in the string.
5. *Write the formal test specification*—This is done by listing the choices within each parameter, as below (the choices have been numbered for reference, but this is not normally the case):

```
Parameters:
  x:
    1) 0       [single]
    2) 1       [property stringok, length1]
    3) 2 - 19  [property stringok, midlength]
    4) 20      [property stringok, length20]
    5) 21      [single]
  a:
    1) length 1       [if stringok and length1]
    2) length 2 - 19  [if stringok and midlength]
    3) length 20      [if stringok and length20]
  c:
    1) At first position in string   [if stringok]
    2) At last position in string [if stringok and not
                                          length1]
```

   3) In middle of string   [if stringok and not
                                              length1]
   4) Not in string   [if stringok]

6. *Create test frames*—Had we not added any constraints we would have
    ended up with 60 (5 × 3 × 4) test frames (and test cases). The addition of
    constraints means that we now have reduced that to 12. For ease of
    reference, the test frames are described using the parameter name and
    the number. They are as follows:

```
x1
x2a1c1
x2a1c4
x3a2c1
x3a2c2
x3a2c3
x3a2c4
x4a3c1
x4a3c2
x4a3c3
x4a3c4
x5
```

7. *Create test cases*—The test cases corresponding to the above frames are
    as follows:

```
x = 0
x = 1, a = 'A', c = 'A'
x = 1, a = 'A', c = 'B'
x = 7, a = 'ABCDEFG', c = 'A'
x = 7, a = 'ABCDEFG', c = 'G'
x = 7, a = 'ABCDEFG', c = 'D'
x = 7, a = 'ABCDEFG', c = 'X'
x = 20, a = 'ABCDEFGHIJKLMNOPQRST', c = 'A'
x = 20, a = 'ABCDEFGHIJKLMNOPQRST', c = 'T'
x = 20, a = 'ABCDEFGHIJKLMNOPQRST', c = 'J'
x = 20, a = 'ABCDEFGHIJKLMNOPQRST', c = 'X'
x = 21
```

Strengths and weaknesses

Criticisms of the technique are that the earlier steps (identifying parameters
and environment conditions, and identifying categories) are not well defined
and rely on the experience of the tester. However, once these stages are
passed then the technique is quite straightforward and the techniques for
test-case reduction make it a useful method for the practitioner.

References

The main reference for the technique is Ostrand and Balcer (1988).

3.2.18 Mutation testing (strong)

Description

Mutation testing is an example of a *fault-based testing* approach—so-called because it is directed towards the possible faults that could occur in a program. It is also sometimes referred to as a measure of test data adequacy, for reasons that will become clear.

The idea is that we take a program and the test data generated for that program (by some means—it does not really matter). The next step is to create a number of *similar* programs, each differing from the original in one small way (i.e. each possessing a *fault*). These programs are called *mutants* of the original. The original test data are then run through the mutant programs. If the test data detect the difference in the mutant program (i.e. they reveal the fault by producing different output from the original program) then the mutant is said to be dead. If, on the other hand, one of the mutants does not produce different results, then this means that the test data are not adequate or sensitive enough to reveal the fault and distinguish the mutant from the original. If this is the case, then the test data need to be examined and augmented to reveal the fault and kill the live mutant.

Of course, there are a very large number of simple faults that could be introduced into a program (estimated to be $O(n^2)$ for an *n*-line program) and so it is recommended to use a subset of possible faults. Budd (1983) recommends the following list as those that are 'indicators of whether the test data is sensitive to small changes in the program'.

- Constant replacement
- Scalar variable replacement
- Scalar variable for constant replacement
- Constant for scalar variable replacement
- Array reference for constant replacement
- Array reference for scalar variable replacement
- Constant for array reference replacement
- Scalar variable for array reference replacement
- Array reference for array reference replacement
- Source constant replacement
- Data statement alteration
- Comparable array name replacement
- Arithmetic operator replacement
- Relational operator replacement
- Logical connector replacement

- Absolute value insertion
- Unary operator insertion
- Statement analysis
- Statement deletion
- Return statement replacement
- GOTO label replacement
- DO statement end replacement

This list is one used in a system for performing mutation tests on FORTRAN programs, but the principles are applicable to other languages.

Given that the changes made to the program are very slight, it is tempting to ask how effective the technique is for more serious or complex errors (such as those not defined by the above list or those involving several statements). To this end, mutation testing makes two assumptions: the competent programmer hypothesis, and the coupling effect. The competent programmer hypothesis states that programmers write programs that are *nearly* correct. That is to say, the faults in the program are only slight. The coupling effect states (DeMillo *et al.*, 1978):

> Test data that distinguishes all programs differing from a correct one by only simple errors is so sensitive that it also implicitly distinguishes more complex errors.

There is some empirical evidence to suggest that the coupling effect exists (Offutt, 1989).

Application

To show how mutation testing may be applied we will start from the basis of having carried out branch testing on our string search example program. We will then concentrate on one section of the program (lines 21 to 29) and show the kind of changes that can be made here and the way that this affects the test data. This segment is shown below:

```
    .
    .
found := FALSE;
i := 1;
while (not(found)) and (i <= x) do
begin
   if a[i] = c then
      found := TRUE
   else
      i := i + 1
end;
    .
    .
```

Table 3.25 Original test data for branch testing

Input				Expected output
x	a	c	response	
25 1	x	x		Input an integer between 1 and 20 Character x appears at position 1
		a	y	Character a does not occur in the string
			n	

As a reminder, the initial set of test data for branch coverage is shown in Table 3.25.

To create our first mutant we will change the line:

```
found := FALSE;
```

to become:

```
found := TRUE;
```

and then re-run our original test data. Note that it is important to only make *one* small change to the program at a time to avoid the danger of introduced faults cancelling each other out. Our test data find this fault by reporting, 'Character a appears at position 1' instead of saying that it does not occur in the string. Mutant 1 is dead.

Mutant 2 replaces the line:

```
i := 1;
```

with:

```
x := 1;
```

Running our original data through this program fails to reveal the fault. Mutant 2 is still live since exactly the same results are output. Analysis of our mutant shows that only the first position in the string will be searched for. We need to increase our string length and search for a character further along it. Our modified test data are shown in Table 3.26. Note that it is important to preserve the effect of earlier tests—we don't want our modified data to fail on mutants that we previously thought dead. The modification modes here are still effective for mutant 1. Mutant 2 is now dead.

Mutant 3 replaces the line:

```
i := 1 + 1;
```

with:

```
i := 1 + 2;
```

Table 3.26 Modified test data to kill mutant 2

Input				Expected output
x	a	c	response	
25 3	xCv	x		Input an integer between 1 and 20 Character x appears at position 1
			y	
		a		Character a does not occur in the string
			y	
		v		Character v appears at position 3
			n	

Once again our test data fail to kill the mutant and we are forced to augment it by searching for the character in the middle of our string. Our modified test data are shown in Table 3.27 and mutant 3 is now dead.

Table 3.27 Modified test data to kill mutant 3

Input				Expected output
x	a	c	response	
25 3	xCv	x		Input an integer between 1 and 20 Character x appears at position 1
			y	
		a		Character a does not occur in the string
			y	
		v		Character v appears at position 3
			y	
		C		Character C appears at position 2
			n	

There are many other changes that could be made to that short section of code—for example, changing the array reference, changing the relational operator and so on. We shall stop creating mutants at this point, hopefully having provided a picture of how the technique works.

There is one more point worth mentioning. Sometimes it is impossible to kill a mutant because no test data can be found that will reveal the fault introduced into the program. In this case, the mutant is regarded as being *equivalent* to the original program. As a slightly absurd illustration of this, consider the following code segment:

```
  .
  .
x := 3;
y := x * 3
if y < 10 then
  .
  .
```

If we were to change the 10 to an 11 then this would make no difference to the operation of the program and no test data could find the fault. It is an equivalent mutant which behaves identically to the original program.

Strengths and weaknesses

One advantage of mutation testing is that it shows the *absence* of particular faults (contrary to Dijkstra's famous comment). By introducing a fault into a program and then showing that test data will reveal it, we know that the fault cannot be there! Furthermore, it does force the programmer to scrutinize and analyse very carefully the program under test in trying to think of test data that will expose a fault he or she has just introduced.

The drawback of mutation testing is that it is computationally expensive to carry out. A very large number of mutant programs can be generated and running test data through each of these, and modifying it if appropriate, is a time-consuming activity. There are systems that can help with the construction of mutants and analysis of results but still some work has to be done by hand.

References

One of the earliest descriptions of mutation testing is to be found in DeMillo *et al.* (1978). Further descriptions are to be found in Budd (1983), which contains overviews of a number of other validation techniques, Wu *et al.* (1988), which bases the technique on syntax direction to increase its practical application, and DeMillo *et al.* (1988), which describes a system to support mutation testing. Woodward and Halewood (1988) introduce a compromise between *strong* and *weak mutation* called *firm mutation*.

3.2.19 Mutation testing (weak)

Originally referred to as 'code-based functional testing'.

Description

Weak mutation testing, as the name suggests, is less demanding than strong mutation testing. The idea is to take some component of a program and create a number of mutants of this component. Test data are then run through the mutants and if, on at least one execution, the results from the mutants and the original are different, then the test data are considered to be adequate. This is best illustrated by an example. Consider a program component involving a Boolean expression such as:

```
if (A and B) or C then
```

and possible mutants:

```
if (A or B) or C then
if (A and B) and C then
if A and (B or C) then
...etc
```

Then, all we need to do is have one run of test data where the original computes different results to the mutants and the data are adequate for mutation testing.

The major difference is that with weak mutation testing it is usually not necessary to actually generate the mutants since the requirements for test data can be determined in advance. Howden (1981) identified the following five function types, or components:

- Data access (or variable reference)
- Data storage (or variable assignment)
- Arithmetic expression
- Arithmetic relation
- Boolean expression

He then developed 'reliable' tests for these—that is, the requirements for test data which would satisfy weak mutation testing. These are described below.

Data access (variable reference): The possible mutants are that a variable is replaced by another variable and so the wrong variable would be referenced. Adequate test data have to ensure the variable has a unique value from all other compatible variables.

Data storage (variable assignment): Again the possible mutant involves variable replacement resulting in the wrong variable holding the value. To detect this, ensure the variable is assigned a new value (different from that previously held).

Arithmetic expressions: Arithmetic expressions are particularly difficult to test since the number of possible mutants is large. Suggestions for generating test data are:

- Ensure different values are taken on by variables.
- Increment each variable value by 1.

- Complement each variable value.
- Result of the expression must be non-zero.

Note that this is only reliable for simple additive and multiplicative errors.

Arithmetic relations (X r Y):   Arithmetic relations can involve two types of mutant: a wrong operator error and a constant error. A wrong operator error is when, rather obviously, the wrong operator has been used (e.g. < instead of ≤) and is tested by checking over a range of operands. A constant error is when a constant 'shift' occurs in one of the operands (for example, x < 3.5 mutates to x < 3.6). The necessary tests are summarized below.

- Wrong operator errors (i.e. 'r' is incorrect). Test on X > Y, X = Y, X < Y
- Constant errors (i.e. detect mutants of the form X r Y + c). The test requirements are similar to those for domain testing and boundary value analysis, and are as follows:

    − r is > or ≤
      X − Y is minimal and > 0
      X − Y is maximal and ≤ 0
    − r is < or ≥
      X − Y is maximal and < 0
      X − Y is minimal and ≥ 0
    − r is = or ≠
      X − Y = 0

Boolean expressions: Mutations of Boolean expressions would involve replacing Boolean operators with compatible equivalents and also negating parts of the expression. To reveal possible mutants it is necessary to generate tests to exercise every combination of the components of the expression. This is equivalent to carrying out *multiple condition coverage*.

It is worth noting that a typical line of code might involve several of the above components. For example, a simple assignment statement:

```
a := b
```

involves variable reference (b) and assignment (a), and the following conditional statement:

```
if ( a = 3 ) or ( b < c − d/4.983)
```

involves arithmetic relations, an arithmetic expression and a Boolean expression.

Application

Applying the technique to our original string searching example and dealing with each component at a time.

Data access (variable reference): It is only necessary to ensure that the variables have unique values from other compatible variables (i.e. those that could replace a variable and still allow it to compile and run). We can therefore deal with the variables type by type.

Character variable references occur on lines 25, 31, 33 and 37. We need to ensure that the array values $a[i]$ are all unique and that the character c has a unique value for at least one execution (i.e. it will not be present in the array). We must also ensure that *response* holds unique values. In addition, we do not want to give any of the characters numeric values (to avoid confusion with the integers).

Integer variable references occur on lines 9, 15, 23, 28 and 31. The variables x and i are closely related (especially on line 15) but we can ensure they have different values in the remainder of the program by giving x a value of 3 and finding the character in the first position.

There is only one Boolean variable so it is bound to have a unique value.

So, our initial test data could be to give x a value of 3, the array a the characters 'aBH', the character c a value of 'a', *response* a value of 'y', c a value of 'x' and, finally, *response* a value of 'n'.

Data storage (variable assignment): Character variable assignments occur on lines 16, 20 and 36. It is essential that these take on new values from the ones that they are currently holding. This is achieved by the data we have so far.

Integer variable assignments occur on lines 8, 12, 15, 22 and 28. We need to give x an initial 'out of range' value, otherwise the rest have been covered by our existing test data.

Boolean variable assignments occur on lines 21 and 26 and have been covered by the existing data.

Arithmetic expressions: The only arithmetic expression occurs on line 28. There is not much we can do to control the values of the variables except ensure that the loop iterates at least twice to increment the values of the variables. Again this is already achieved.

Arithmetic relations: Arithmetic relations occur on lines 9 and 23. For line 9, letting x have value 0, 1, 2, 19, 20 and 21 would satisfy the requirements for both wrong operator errors and constant errors. In line 23, failing to find a character in the string would ensure that x was less than i, equal to i and greater than i. Again this achieves the requirements for both types of errors.

Table 3.28 Weak mutation testing for decision on line 9

(x < 1) or (x > 20)		Test data
T	T	Impossible
T	F	$x = 0$
F	T	$x = 21$
F	F	$x = 1$

Table 3.29 Weak mutation testing for decision on line 23

(not(found))	and	(i <= x)	Test requirements
T		T	*True* on entry
T		F	Character not found in string
F		T	Character found in string
F		F	Impossible

Table 3.30 Weak mutation testing for decision on line 37

(response = 'n')	or	(response = 'N')	Test data
T		T	Impossible
T		F	'n'
F		T	'N'
F		F	'y' (or anything but 'n' or 'N')

Boolean expressions: Boolean expressions occur on lines 9, 23 and 37. As was stated earlier, the test requirements for Boolean expressions are the same as for multiple condition coverage. These requirements are shown in Table 3.28. Lines 23 and 37 are shown in Tables 3.29 and 3.30.

The complete set of test data to achieve weak mutation testing is shown in Table 3.31. Note that values for the second, third, fourth and fifth sets of data (separated by the double horizontal line) are quite arbitrary. All we are concerned with is generating a value of 'N' for *response*. Similarly, we do not care about what testing we do with strings of 19 and 20 characters. They are there as a limit test and all other test requirements have been met (although common sense might tell us to search for the last character in the string).

Strengths and weaknesses

The strength of weak mutation is that, like strong mutation, it promotes a thorough analysis of the program under test but is computationally much cheaper. Furthermore, it is not necessary to physically generate all the mutants.

Table 3.31 Test data for weak mutation testing

Input				Expected output
x	a	c	*response*	
21				Input an integer between 1 and 20
0				Input an integer between 1 and 20
3	aBH	a		Character a appears at position 1
			y	
		x		Character x does not occur in the string
			n	
1	x	x		Character x appears at position 1
			N	
2	Wx	x		Character x appears at position 2
			N	
19	abc...qrs	A		Character A does not occur in the string
			n	
20	abc...rst	t		Character t appears at position 20
			N	

The major weakness is that unlike strong mutation testing, it is not reliable for the program as a whole. By this it is meant that although a fault in a component may be revealed by test data, when adequate weak mutation test data are applied to the whole program, the fault may remain hidden so the program (incorrectly) computes the correct output. This means that the adequacy of the data is local to the component under test.

Howden (1982b) considers weak mutation to be a refinement of branch testing. That is, it forces branch testing but also tests other simple components of fault-revealing data. Indeed, because of the test requirements it imposes on Boolean expressions, it can be thought of as a refinement of *multiple condition coverage*.

In a comparative small experimental evaluation on Fortran programs, Girgis and Woodward (1986) found that weak mutation testing was outperformed by dataflow testing, which in turn was outperformed by control flow testing (especially LCSAJs). However, they did find that some of the seeded faults were not found by all techniques and advocated that techniques should be used in combination rather than in isolation.

References

The earliest description of weak mutation testing is to be found in Howden (1981) and refined in Howden (1982b). A system to support the technique is described in Girgis and Woodward (1985).

3.3 BUT WHICH ONE SHOULD I USE?

Sadly, this is a question that is not easy to answer. The large number of testing techniques developed is not supported by a large body of empirical evidence describing the relative merits of each technique. One possible reason for this is the problem of repeatability. Many of the techniques are not prescriptive in their selection of test data, and so different users of the technique will choose different test data (one set of which may reveal faults that the other misses). For this reason, any empirical study needs a fairly large sample of representative users even to begin drawing conclusions based on statistical evidence.

However, some experimental studies have been carried out and this section reports the results of a few of these. Hetzel (1976) compared the effectiveness of requirements-based testing methods (test cases are constructed strictly from the program specification) with the effectiveness of code reading (programmers inspect the code manually) and mixed testing (the construction of tests is based on the specification and on the code). He found that the two testing techniques caught roughly the same percentage of errors, and outperformed the code reading.

Howden (1978) compared path testing, branch testing and functional requirements-based testing. In this study, functional testing found 61 per cent of the errors, path testing found 43 per cent and branch testing found 21 per cent. Howden notes, though, that some of the faults found by path testing were not found by functional testing.

Basili and Selby (1987) looked at code reading, functional testing (using equivalence partitioning and boundary value analysis) and statement testing. They experimented using four different software systems and a variety of programmer expertise. They found that, among the professional programmers, code reading detected more faults and had a higher fault detection rate than both functional and statement testing. Functional testing discovered more faults than statement testing, but the detection rate was the same. Among the less-experienced programmers, in one group statement testing was outperformed by the other techniques, and in the other group no difference was found. Code reading detected more interface faults and functional testing detected more control faults.

Lauterbach and Randall (1989) compared branch testing, functional testing, random testing and some static analysis techniques including code reviews. On average, code reviews were found to be most effective, but in many instances were outperformed by branch testing. Of the testing techniques, the highest coverage level was achieved by branch coverage.

The four summaries above are in many ways typical of other experiments in that they highlight the difficulties associated with carrying out empirical evaluations of testing techniques. The results are not consistent and frequently it is different methods under comparison. On top of that, many of the results depend on the expertise of the participant, the type of software under test, and the type and distribution of faults in the software. More studies, well-controlled and well-executed, are desperately required, however.

Another approach to comparison is a more theoretical one based on the relative coverage achieved by the different techniques (note that a higher coverage level does not guarantee a higher fault detection rate). On this basis we are able to create a partial ordering of the techniques where techniques that subsume others are placed higher up in the ordering. By subsume, we mean that: given two testing techniques *A* and *B*, then, if by generating test data for *A* we have achieved the necessary criteria for generating data for *B*, the *A* subsumes *B*. For example, generating test data to achieve branch coverage means that we will also achieve statement coverage, therefore branch coverage subsumes statement coverage. Ntafos (1988) compares a number of techniques (many of them data flow based) in this way and a subset of this partial ordering is shown in Fig. 3.21. Note, that we are unable to say anything about the related merits of LCSAJs or data flow testing.

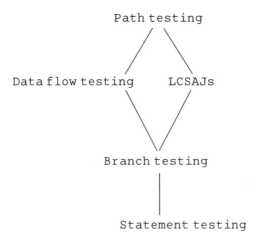

Figure 3.21   Partial ordering of coverage criteria (© 1988, IEEE).

Further interesting, and provocative examinations of many structural testing techniques are to be found in Weyuker and Jeng (1991), and Hamlet and Taylor (1990).

3.4 SUPPORTING SOFTWARE TOOLS

There are in existence a number of tools that assist in the testing process (see NCC (1989) or Lutz (1990)). However, there are pitifully few that assist in the real testing problem—the creation of test data and corresponding expected results. The basic reason for this is that the generation of tests to cause the execution of an arbitrary path in a program is an undecidable problem. In this section it is useful to widen our perspective and also consider those tools that are test *data* generators (that is, no corresponding expected results are calculated), in order to gain an insight into the generation of test cases. DeMillo *et al.* (1987) classify test data generation tools into three categories: pathwise test data generators, data specification systems and random test data generators. It is worth considering each of these in turn.

3.4.1 Pathwise test data generators

The tools in this class follow a similar approach to the generation of test data. The program is viewed as a directed graph. A path is chosen through this graph and is symbolically executed (a non-trivial exercise presenting problems with loops, arrays, module calls and infeasible paths) in order to give a predicate for that path (the conjunction of the predicates along the path) which defines a subset of the input space. Choosing values from this input space will cause this path to be taken. If no value can be found then it is indicative of contradictory predicates and an unexecutable path. Even if the path is executable, the path predicates will either be linear or non-linear. If they are linear then linear programming techniques may be applied to solve them and thus find a value to follow that path. If they are non-linear then the problem is more difficult and it is necessary to use non-linear programming techniques, often coupled with heuristics to increase efficiency. It is problems such as these that have thwarted the large-scale development of tools for the automatic generation of test data. Examples of such systems are ATDG (Hoffman, 1975), ATTEST (Clarke, 1979), RETS (Ihm and Ntafos, 1983) and SETAR (Kundu, 1979). Korel (1990) provides some recent advances in this area.

3.4.2 Data specification systems

These systems generate test data from a language describing the input data. The user (tester) writes a description of the input data of the software under test and then quantities of test data conforming to this description are generated. One example of this approach is systems that take as their input grammatical descriptions of a language (there are a number of papers which look at the use of grammars to generate test data—see Duncan (1978) and Maurer (1990), for example) and generate programs from this description in order to test compilers (e.g. GENTEXTS (Houghton, 1982)). Another example is that taken by TESTGEN (NCC, 1989) which creates test input sequences for finite state machines (e.g. entity life histories described by SSADM). Less sophisticated systems are those that generate test data from descriptions of the input files. One drawback of using such an approach in isolation is that large quantities of test data might be generated which only exercise a small percentage of the code.

3.4.3 Random test data generators

Test data for each input to the program are generated randomly according to different profiles. One approach is to distribute the data over the different path domains in the program, another is to distribute data according to a user profile (if it is available), thus simulating the likely usage of the software. While this approach addresses the drawbacks of data specification systems and is an attractively simple process, most supporting tools are only in the development stages.

3.4.4 Other tools

The above list of categories is not comprehensive since it does not cater for tools that generate test data from specifications. In some ways it could be argued that the second category (data specification systems) covers this, but specifications do more than describe the permissible data—they also describe the necessary processing associated with that data. There are a number of tools and methods that generate test data from specifications and these deserve further consideration. One approach taken by Choquet (1986) and Bougé et al. (1986) is to generate test data sets from algebraic data type specifications implemented in Prolog or extensions thereof. Prolog is also used by Hoffman and Strooper (1991) to write test scripts for testing C code. Another system, DAISTS (Gannon et al., 1981), combines a data abstraction implementation language with specification by algebraic axioms. It compiles a program consisting of the axioms as a test driver for the implementing code. Data points are fed into this program to determine if the implementation and axioms agree. The axioms eliminate the need for an oracle and the testing is automatic. DeMillo and Offutt (1991) have also developed a substantial toolset to support the technique of mutation testing. However, perhaps the most popular class of tools for assisting in the testing process are the dynamic analysers. There are a large number of these on the market (TestBed from LDRA, Logiscope from Verilog, and Cantata and AdaTEST from IPL, to mention just a few). These instrument the program (by inserting probes—function calls) at various points in the program (after every branch, for example). When the program is run with test data the probes are 'activated' and a measure is gained of such things as the percentage of statements executed or branches covered. Consider the segment of code below:

```
while x < 3 do
if y > 107.8 then
   z := z + 1
else
   z := z - 3;
```

If this was subjected to dynamic analysis then probes would have to be inserted and the semantics of the program retained. Different analysers work in different ways, but one solution might be as follows:

```
while x < 3 do
begin
   probe1(..);
   if y > 107.8 then
   begin
     probe2(..);
     z := z + 1
   end
   else
   begin
     probe3(..);
     z := z - 3
   end
end;
```

The program is then run with the probes inserted. The number of probes executed (and the number of times) gives a measure of how thoroughly the program has been tested.

Dynamic analysers are built along the same principles as static analysers and are just as vulnerable when it comes to vagaries of syntax in non-standard language implementations. Further difficulties are caused by the presence of infeasible paths. These are routes through the program which, due to particular combinations of conditions, can never be executed, and have a great effect on the figures relating to percentage of statement or branches executed (coverage should be reported in percentage of feasible statements, branches, etc. covered). Some infeasible paths can be detected statically (i.e. without execution of the program) but many are not detectable automatically. See Hedley and Hennell (1985) for more information on this subject.

4

TESTING THROUGH THE LIFE-CYCLE

The aim of this chapter is to examine how testing may be applied to different artefacts produced throughout the systems development life-cycle. In particular it tries to show how the testing methods described may be applied, and so deliberately leaves out other more 'traditional' quality assurance techniques such as walkthroughs. In addition this chapter aims to show how implementation paradigms other than the (relatively) straight-forward, sequential imperative that we have already considered, may be tested.

Testing is most suited to the executable artefact. However, much of the output from the systems development process is *not* executable. As a consequence of this the material is usually subjected to other forms of scrutiny, or even ignored except as input to a later stage of development. As we shall see, much of the development material provides a rich source of test data. This test data may be used in two ways:

- As input to reviews/walkthroughs of subsequent development stages. This may be used to check consistency and completeness between stages.
- As test data to the corresponding executable artefact. So, just as test data derived from a specification may be used to test an implementation, so test data from a design may be used for integration testing, test data from the analysis stages may be used to test the system and test data from requirements may be used to define the acceptance tests.

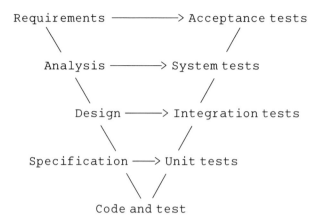

Figure 4.1 Idealized systems development life-cycle.

This is shown diagrammatically in Fig. 4.1.

There is another benefit to carrying out testing at these earlier stages. The very activity of generating test data forces a close examination of the product which in itself may reveal faults. Furthermore, if testing proves to be particularly difficult, then what are the subsequent development stages going to be like? This may be an early indication of an inelegant and poorly designed product.

I am aware that the definition of requirements, analysis and design is cloudy and may vary between individuals. In this book, the requirements are the initial statements concerning *what* the software should do. The analysis documents look at how the requirements may be logically achieved. The design stages are the realization of the analysis stages in software and involve, among other things, fitting a structure to the software.

4.1 ANALYSIS OF REQUIREMENTS

The requirements are obviously the most important product of the software engineering activity since every other activity is based on these requirements. An error made at this stage is going to have a devastating effect on the remainder of the product.

Natural language is an extremely popular medium for writing requirements. It is widely known and understood, and its flexibility and expressive power means that complex requirements can be expressed without too much difficulty. However, this expressive power, as everyone knows, also leads to its downfall—ambiguity. On top of this it is very hard to ensure that natural language requirements are complete (in that the whole of the system has been specified).

4.1.1 Testability

Before going on to test our natural language requirements we have to ensure that the requirements are testable. That is, it is possible to devise a test to check whether the requirements have been met. If this cannot be done, then there is no way of checking whether or not the requirement has been dealt with by the system. Classic examples of untestable requirements are phrases like, 'The system should be user-friendly', or, 'The response time should be reasonable'. These are so imprecise as to be of no use to the tester (or the developer). The phrase 'user-friendly' has different meanings to different people. What one person might find to be a reasonable response time, another might find agonizingly slow.

The easiest way to filter out such requirements is to attempt to write acceptance tests from them that may be answered 'Yes' or 'No'. So, instead of a 'reasonable' response time we might have something like, 'The response time is less that 1.5 seconds for 95 per cent of the time under average system loading'. In this way it is easier for us to design tests and also possible for the independent observer to evaluate the results.

4.1.2 Testing requirements

When testing requirements we want to ensure that the requirement is present in the implemented system. Therefore, the lowest level of requirements testing we could do is to generate test data to test every requirement at least once (a 'statement test' of requirements, if you like). However, we want to use the techniques we have described to create tests that are a little more demanding. While testing every requirement individually forms a good basic acceptance test, we wish to apply a little more stress to the system by examining the limits and combinations of the requirements. Frequently, the way in which requirements are expressed does not make them suitable for application in any of the structural techniques. On the other hand, the functional techniques are very easily applied (after all, this is what many were designed for).

The use of equivalence partitioning allows us to examine requirements in more detail (dealing with different ranges and values of data, for example) and restrain the number of possible test cases. We can apply boundary value analysis to many of the requirements to examine their behaviour at the limits of their specified range.

Another technique that is applicable is cause–effect graphing. This is an attractive technique at this stage since it tests the interaction between requirements. Similarly, category–partition testing is a powerful technique at this stage since it looks at both combinations and limits of data. In addition, the high level of abstraction means that we are less at risk of encountering a combinatorial explosion (especially if we handle distinct groups of requirements separately, and treat requirements in a hierarchical fashion).

4.2 THE ANALYSIS STAGES

In the idealized life-cycle shown in Fig. 4.1, the test data from the analysis stages are going to contribute towards the system tests. We shall examine the following representations of requirements (and their analysis): natural language, data flow diagrams, entity–relationship diagrams and entity–life histories.

4.2.1 Data flow diagrams

Introduction

Data flow diagrams are a very common technique for analysing (and subsequently designing) a system. Given that data flow diagrams are so popular, and also well supported by a number of CASE tools, it is somewhat surprising that the method provides very little by way of support for testing, and that very few testing techniques have been developed to integrate with this notation. In fact, data flow diagrams do not readily lend themselves to the generation of test data. The main reason for this is that they tend to be very hierarchical, with the resolution of ambiguity occurring at the lowest level. This problem is illustrated in Fig. 4.2.

One tactic for testing such a data flow diagram would be to select an input flow and trace this through to determine the corresponding output. So, we start at the highest level and, to determine what the output should be, descend to the next level of the hierarchy. We then try to trace the flow through this level and find we have to descend to the next level. This continues until we reach the process specifications at the bottom level (it is here that any ambiguity is resolved). Then we move up through the hierarchy until we finally emerge at the top level with the answer. This is a very simple case. In reality the flow would be split up at the lower levels and we would have to trace a number of flows up and down the hierarchy until we could finally reassemble them to give the final output. Trying to perform such a task by hand is not only laborious, but also error prone.

The approach taken by McCabe and Schulmeyer (1985) is to test all the major functions in the system. The functions are identified and a 'trace' is made of all the processes (bubble numbers) contributing to this function. This approach relies heavily on the tester having an understanding of the semantics of the system and being able to identify the major functions.

Data flow testing

Since it is a data flow diagram being tested, it would seem sensible to examine the application of the data flow testing approach. When applied to programs, a data flow-based testing approach is concerned with definitions and usage of data. This approach transfers neatly to data flow diagrams,

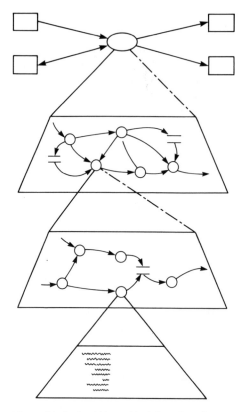

Figure 4.2 Stylized hierarchical data flow diagram.

where we are modelling the transformation of data and most of the functionality of the diagram is concerned with defining and referencing data. Often, data flow diagrams will reference data more than they will define them and these references are not as independent as references to variables in a program (i.e. one reference will depend on another reference, and so on). So we frequently end up with a definition and a 'chain' of references. Figure 4.3 shows the possible ways in which data may be defined and referenced within a diagram. So, A is defined at terminator (1) and at process (4), and referenced at process (2) and at terminator (5). B is defined at process (2) and referenced at process (4), and C is defined at process (2) and referenced at processes (3) and (4).

There are a couple of initial problems with this technique which need to be resolved. Firstly, data within a diagram does not remain in one simple form. It may be split into a number of smaller data items and combined into larger data items. The simplest way to cope with this is to develop the tests for just one data item at a time and start with the simplest items. Consider the example in Fig. 4.4.

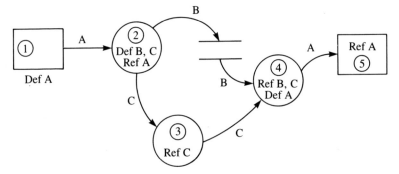

Figure 4.3 Definitions and references in a data flow diagram.

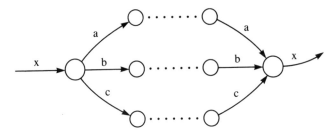

Figure 4.4 Flow split and merge in a data flow diagram.

In order to be able to generate the tests for x, we need first to consider generating tests for a, b and c. Sometimes, a data flow may appear only once, between two bubbles (i.e. one defines it and the other references it), but we still need to be sure that we generate tests to exercise this data flow.

Secondly, we need to address the point about levels. The solution is similar. Because the simplest data items usually occur at the lowest levels, we generate tests for the lowest levels first, and then move on up the hierarchy.

Of course, when we talk about 'generating tests' at this stage we tend to mean generating test requirements, or criteria, rather than the actual test data. So, for the abstract example above, we know we want some data that will cause x to be defined and later referenced at that point in the diagram. There will tend to be a large number of actual data values that will do this.

So, for our abstract example in Fig. 4.3, we can identify the points at which each data item is defined and referenced (the numbers refer to the processes or terminators in the diagram) as follows:

```
A :  1,2   B :  2,4   C :  2,3
     1,5               2,4
     4,5               3,4
```

All that is then required is to generate test data to cause the feasible pairs to be executed.

A purely structural approach

The data flow approach described above is suitable for testing the transformation of data from input to output at any level in the hierarchy. If we want to concentrate on just one function, or 'bubble' in the data flow diagram, we can take a structural approach to the testing. The structural approach ensures that at least every data item is sent to the process, and every data item is generated by the process. This tactic is good if we can isolate the function within the system, or if it has been modified and we only want to update part of the test suite. However, as an approach for testing an entire system, it rapidly becomes unwieldy and over-complex, with the added drawback that it generates a large number of infeasible paths through the system.

So, for the processes in Fig. 4.3 we would need to generate test data that caused process (2) to read A and generate B and C, process (3) to read B and generate B, and process (4) to read B and C and generate A.

4.2.2 Entity–relationship diagrams

The use of data flow diagrams generates data that tend to conform to the intended model. As a consequence we have not generated test data that make much use of boundary values or are in any way likely to find faults by stretching the system.

Entity–relationship diagramming is an approach to data modelling which describes the relationships between the major data items (entities) in the system. Consider the example of a library. The library has a number of registered borrowers and a number of books. Each borrower is able to borrow a number of books. This is shown in Fig. 4.5. We say that there is a one–many relationship between library and borrowers (that is, for one library, there are many borrowers). This one–many relationship also holds

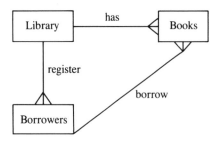

Figure 4.5 Example entity–relationship diagram.

for library and books, and borrowers and books. Other permissible relationships are one–one, many–one and many–many. We can use the principle of boundary-value analysis to test the limits of these relationships by examining the combinations between them. We can start by having a library with one book and one borrower who borrows the one book. We can then test what happens if the one borrower tries to borrow n books (n is undefined but signifies 'many' (i.e., more than one!). Other combinations may be similarly examined. We can also look at 'illegal' tests such as zero books.

The same principles can be applied to examine the combinations between entities in larger diagrams. Of course, it may not be physically possible to generate data (for acceptance testing) for some of the illegal relationship but the scenarios can still be useful for reviews of subsequent stages.

4.2.3 Entity–life histories—an object-oriented approach

If we view the system in an object-oriented fashion then our attention is immediately focused on the data (as opposed to the functions) within the system. One approach to object-oriented design (Ince, 1991) uses entity–life histories to identify the objects in a system and the methods that are going to act upon them. Entity–life histories (ELHs) model the actions suffered and performed by an entity in a system. They use hierarchical JSP-type (Jackson, 1975) diagrams which have symbols for expressing selection (o), iteration (*) and backtracking (!).

As an example, consider the life history of the book entity in a library. It is purchased, placed on the shelf, and eventually disposed of. While it is on the shelf it may be borrowed any number of times (from zero to many). It is disposed of by either selling it or throwing it away. This life history is shown in Fig. 4.6.

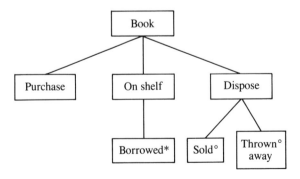

Figure 4.6 Entity–life history for library book.

Carrying out a simple top-to-bottom, left-to-right traversal of the diagram generates the different possible life histories that the entity may have. These are expressed in terms of the leaf nodes and are as follows:

```
1) Purchased, Borrowed 0 times, Sold
2) Purchased, Borrowed n times, Sold
3) Purchased, Borrowed 0 times, Thrown away
4) Purchased, Borrowed n times, Thrown away
```

We could examine 'Borrowed n times' further by breaking it down into 'Borrowed once' and 'Borrowed many times'. Once again we need to generate test data that conform to these criteria. See Roper and Smith (1987) for related work to this.

4.3 DESIGN

Whereas the earlier stages of requirements and analysis generated tests that are used for acceptance and system tests (as well as input to subsequent reviews and walkthroughs), test data from designs are going to be used for carrying out integration tests. This is a natural mapping, since a design is imposing some form of modular structure on the results of the analysis for the purposes of making the construction of the system feasible. It is in the design that the communication between modules is defined and it is this communication that we wish to examine in the integration testing stage. The design notation we are going to use is a fairly standard one which defines the relationship between modules in a system by showing the calling structure and the data flow.

When carrying out an integration test we want to adopt an incremental strategy. It is very unlikely that a 'big bang' approach (attempting to put all the modules in a system together in one go, rather than trying to assemble a smaller subsystem first) will succeed, and if it does not, then trying to locate and isolate faults is extremely difficult. Such an incremental strategy follows:

1. Select a module and call it in the simplest way possible. This is a simple test and may not use all the module's parameters.
2. Call the module using all its parameters (if possible) or ensure that all parameters have been used in previous tests.
3. Call the module from all other 'directly' linked modules using all parameters. This tests the module's response to calls from all possible places in the system. So, in the diagram in Fig. 4.7, we would want to call C from A and B since up to this point we would have been using either A or B.
4. Using the data flow testing approach detailed for data flow diagrams,

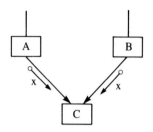

Figure 4.7 Example module calling structure.

test longer call structures by examining the paths that a data item can take around the system. In this way we link several modules together in a way similar to that in which they will be used.

The four-stage strategy described allows a cautious incremental approach which eventually leads to the construction of longer chains of calls based upon the passage of data around the system (and therefore the likely usage of the system).

For a further examination of the subject of integration testing, the reader is directed towards the work of Haley and Zweben (1984) and Harrold and Soffa (1991).

4.4 SPECIFICATIONS

Tests derived from specifications form our traditional 'black box', or functional test cases. Their use is to test the implementation of whatever was specified without reference to the implementation. The specification is usually the lowest-level document given to the programmer and may vary greatly between organizations. In some places, the specification may be highly detailed, so that implementation merely becomes coding with little in the way of design decisions to be made. Here, the specification might result in one module, or a small number of highly related functions (depending on the implementation language). In others, the specification may be at a much higher level, with the programmer making the majority of implementation-related decisions. This larger gulf between the specification and the implementation would result in the production of a larger number of modules or functions.

4.4.1 Natural language

Many specifications are still written in natural language. The main contenders here for generating test data are the 'traditional' functional testing techniques of equivalence partitioning, boundary value analysis, cause–effect graphing and category–partition testing.

4.4.2 Structured English

Structured English is again a common specification technique. The idea is to express the specification in a high-level pseudo-code that is easy to read and understand, but removes many of the problems of ambiguity in natural language. Its critics would say that its algorithmic nature is too strongly suggestive of a solution and makes decisions that should be in the hands of the implementer. An example Structured English representation of our string searching program might be:

```
read valid number
read string
  repeat
  read a character
  if character is in string then
    print its position
  else
    print message saying character not found
until no more characters to be searched for
```

A structural approach

It is because of this algorithmic form that Structured English is a powerful medium for generating test data. Its program-like appearance means that the techniques developed for source-code are applicable to a specification expressed in this form. Furthermore, the specifications tend to be much shorter than programs so the application of more rigorous and demanding structural testing techniques is facilitated. With similar ease we could also apply stronger structural coverage techniques such as data flow or LCSAJs which would cause such things as null iterations of the loops.

Domain testing and partition analysis

Another interesting and appealing feature about Structured English is the simplicity of the notation used. While the lack of formality or rigidly defined syntax and semantics can admittedly cause problems, the notation and level of abstraction mean that we do not have to (or *want* to) use such constructs as arrays or pointers. The consequence of this is that many of the problems associated with data flow analysis of programs (when trying to perform a symbolic execution, for example) disappear. This means that the techniques of domain testing and partition analysis are readily applicable to Structured English specifications.

Fault-based testing

The fault-based techniques of mutation testing can be brought into play at the specification stage. By introducing small faults in the specification we can detect if our test data is sensitive enough to reveal these. In a similar way to the application to programs, these can be applied to the procedural, Structured English specifications.

4.4.3 Formal specifications

There have been suggestions that the use of formal methods removes the necessity for testing by proving the equivalence between a specification and implementation. However, factors such as the difficulties in carrying out proofs, the representation of data in the underlying machine, and the sometimes imprecise semantics of programming languages mean that only the foolhardy would not test out the final implementation. Perhaps contrary to their aims, the developers of formal methods have provided us with some excellent material for testing.

Consider a VDM (Jones, 1986) type of specification for the process of checking how many copies of a library book are in stock:

```
Bfile = map classno to quantity
CHECK-STOCK(Bookno : classno) : Quant : Z
ext rd Book-File : Bfile
pre Bookno ∈ dom Book-File
post Quant = Book-File(Bookno)
```

This defines a file that is a mapping from the classification number of the book to the quantity. The function then takes a book number (of type class number), checks that it is on the file and, if it is, returns the corresponding quantity.

The excellent point about a specification like this (from the testing point of view) is that the post-condition provides an *oracle*. There is no need for us to calculate what the expected output is going to be—it is already done for us. Providing the input conforms to the pre-condition, the output will conform to the post-condition.

A very straightforward test would then involve just generating any data that conformed to the pre-condition and checking that the output conformed to the post-condition.

Functional testing

Formal state-based specifications like VDM allow the application of our 'standard' functional testing techniques. We can select equivalence classes and boundaries according to the information supplied in the pre- and post-conditions. We must take care not to generate equivalence classes that fall outside the pre-condition, since the output from such a case is undefined. The only time that we can do this is when testing a number of specifications whose pre-conditions cover a domain under test and where data that does not meet one pre-condition will be 'caught' by another.

Domain testing and partition analysis

Structural techniques in general are tricky to apply to specifications of this nature since there is no sense of data flow or processing (or very little, anyway). Hall and Hierons (1991) have investigated the testing of several 'formal' specification techniques. The formal specification makes the application of the partition and domain techniques (to the specification, anyway) even simpler than in the case of Structured English. No longer do we have to carry out a symbolic execution of the specification—the pre- and post-conditions have already done this since they define the relationships between the inputs and the outputs. In VDM specifications, the pre-condition defines the input domain and the post-condition may further sub-partition this domain.

Fault-based testing

The mutation-type approaches can be applied to formal specifications. We can make slight changes to the specification (such as changing the 'variable' names, or the computations) and then ensure that the data we have generated are sensitive enough to catch the faults. This technique has also been applied to algebraic specifications by Woodward (1989) and others.

4.5 IMPLEMENTATION

We have seen in our description of testing methods how they may be applied to serial, imperative programs. In this section we will consider how the techniques may be applied to concurrent, object-oriented and declarative paradigms.

4.5.1 Concurrent

In testing concurrent programs we are concerned both about the results they calculate (or processes performed) and about their interaction with other processes. This section will concentrate on the latter; the former can be tested using any of the other methods. We want to try and find if there are any faults that may be revealed by causing processes to interact in particular ways. We can examine the principles of this using the Ada tasking model. Consider the example of a very small (one item) buffer running as a task with a number of other tasks writing characters to it and reading characters from it. An outline Ada implementation of this now follows:

```
task minibuf is
  entry buf_write(x: in item);
  entry buf_read(x: out item);
end;

task body minibuf is
  y : item;
begin
  loop
    accept buf_write(x: in item) do
      y := x;
    end buf_write;
    accept buf_read(x: out item);
      x := y;
    end buf_read;
  end loop;
end minibuf;
```

This is used by a number of other tasks that would have the following rough structure:

```
task task1 is
  .
  .
  minibuf.buf_write(anitem)
  .
  .
end task1

task task2 is
  .
  .
  minibuf.buf_write(anitem)
  .
  .
end task2

task task3 is
  .
  .
  minibuf.buf_read(anitem)
  .
  .
end task3
```

```
task task4 is
    .
    .
    minibuf.buf_read(anitem)
    .
    .
end task4
```

In other words, we have a number of tasks simultaneously trying to write to and read from the same data (an item of some sort). To test this access, we find that the data flow testing method comes in useful. We should attempt to test all interactions of data items that are accessed concurrently. The diagram in Fig. 4.8 shows how the data item is defined and used in the system.

So, we can see that in the interaction among modules the item is defined in task1 and task2 and referenced by task3 and task4. We would then generate test data to test the four possible interactions among these modules, namely

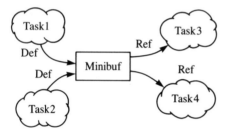

Figure 4.8 Structure of task interaction.

task1–task3, task1–task4, task2–task3 and task2–task4. We could also examine the illegal interactions of task1–task2, task2–task1, task3–task4 and task4–task3.

For further information on the subject of testing concurrent software see, for example, Brinch Hansen (1978), Tai (1989), Yang and Chung (1990), and Taylor *et al.* (1992).

4.5.2 Object oriented

Object-oriented implementations (see Ince (1991) for a good overview of the subject) present a number of interesting problems for the tester. The tying of a number of methods (procedures) to a data item should make the testing simpler. This is because the procedures will act only on the data item and communicate with the 'outside world' using parameters and so the scope for side-effects is reduced. Furthermore, the procedures will tend to be simple, performing very distinct functions. This means that the application of any of the testing methods described is relatively straightforward. On top of this, the use of inheritance to base objects on other (previously tested) objects, and to introduce a small number of other methods related to that new object, means that we can build and test systems in a controlled fashion.

In an interesting discussion of testing object-oriented programs, Perry and Kaiser (1990) show that all is not as simple as the above paragraph suggests. They argue that features such as encapsulation actually compound the testing necessary and inheritance hides dependencies that would be easier to test if they were made explicit. They use four of Weyuker's 11 test data adequacy axioms (Weyuker, 1988a) to examine the problems involved in testing object-oriented programs.

Consider the concept of *encapsulation*—the separation of interface and implementation. Received wisdom has it that if the implementation is changed then only the implementation need be retested. Perry and Kaiser argue that the *anticomposition* axiom (adequately testing two components in isolation is insufficient to test the entire system—composing two components results in an interaction that cannot occur in isolation) suggests that all dependent units should be tested. In other words, it is always necessary to repeat integration tests. Furthermore, the *antidecomposition* axiom (which states that testing a component in the context of an enclosing program may not be adequate for other uses of the component) means that the addition of a new subclass requires the testing of all other components derived from the same parent (they now exist in a new context).

The introduction of local methods that take precedence over (override) inherited ones with the same name require different sets of data. This is because they might compute the same function in a slightly different way. This concept is captured by the *anti-extensionality* axiom.

The *general multiple change* axiom states that if two programs are syntactically similar (one can be transformed into the other by changing relational operators, arithmetic operators or constants) then they will require different test sets. This applies to *multiple inheritance* where different components may have arisen through different routes.

A further problem arises, however, when we consider the notion of polymorphism. This allows objects to be instantiated for a variety of different data types. So, while we may have tested an object over the domain of integers or characters, the instantiation of a new object for real numbers or a user-defined type has effectively not been tested. In other words, we cannot extend the results of testing over one data type to another. The only solution to this is to test over the entire range of possible data types.

Further examinations of the subject of testing object-oriented software may be found in the work of Harrold *et al.* (1992) and Smith and Robson (1990).

4.5.3 Declarative languages and knowledge-based systems

As has been mentioned before, the testing techniques described in this book have been applied mainly to 'vanilla' systems. That is, those constructed according to well-defined and accepted techniques and implemented using a sequential imperative language. This is not to say that these systems are not complex.

One area that has seen especially little in the way of application of traditional testing techniques is that of declarative languages and knowledge-based systems. Declarative languages, such as Prolog, are very different from the imperative paradigm. They are set out in terms of goals and subgoals necessary to achieve that goal. There is little semblance of a traditional structure as in procedural languages since the evaluation is controlled by an interpreter or compiler. A very simplistic view of a knowledge-based system is shown in Fig. 4.9.

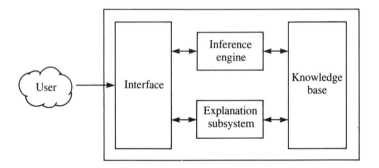

Figure 4.9 Main components of a knowledge-based system.

There are a number of factors that make knowledge-based systems particularly hard to test:

- The structure of the knowledge base tends to be non-procedural which means that the concept of a 'path' or 'branch' (so familiar in structural testing) is not obvious, and may be absent altogether.
- The systems are evolutionary in nature. They may 'learn' from exposure to different examples and update the knowledge base accordingly.
- It may not be a straightforward task to classify the output as right or wrong. Indeed, the output may fall into a number of classes such as ideal, acceptable, unacceptable and so on. Furthermore there is the problem of bias in the interpretation of results—the person testing the system might not actually agree with what the system suggests!

There is also the problem of finding actual test cases. While the requirements and design documents may be used to generate tests, the very existence of a knowledge-based system means that it has to be tested on realistic data and its output verified by a human expert. Any data used in development cannot be used since it might prejudice the results (the system presumably will deal with such instances correctly since it 'knows' about them).

A further complication is deciding what to validate in a system which contains such diverse components. It is argued (O'Keefe *et al.*, 1991) that it is insufficient to examine just the final results and that it is the reasoning process that has to be checked. The reason for this is that poor reasoning will not scale up to produce correct results on a large problem despite being apparently correct on a small example (it is analogous to checking a child's mathematical ability by looking at their answers to a test and paying no attention to the approach they have taken to attempt to solve the problem). It is argued that the inference engine is just another piece of software (frequently written in a procedural language) and should be tested as such.

Consider the following example which has a number of facts representing a family tree (shown in diagrammatic form beside the rules) and a rule defining the grandparent relation.

```
parent(ann,bob).
parent(alec,bob).
parent(ann,billy).
parent(alec,billy).
parent(billy,clare).
parent(brenda,clare).

grandparent(X,Y):-
   parent(X,Z),parent(Z,Y).
```

```
ann + alec
   /      \
  /        \
bob    billy + brenda
             |
           clare
```

In testing such a system we can take a number of approaches. We can employ structural testing analogies such as statement testing to generate test data to use every clause in the knowledge base. Similarly we can try and exercise every rule, or every branch of every rule, and so on. However, this technique is fairly limited in its scope—when a large number of rules exist there is not always an obvious 'path' through them and so coverage measures tend to be limited to single rules.

We can also employ the fault-based techniques of mutation testing. So we could make changes to the rules and then determine whether or not our test data was adequate to detect these changes. Changes to be made could include changing operators from *and* to *or* as shown below:

```
grandparent(X,Y):-
   parent(X,Z);parent(Z,Y).
```

or swapping variables in the facts:

```
grandparent(X,Y):-
  parent(X,Z);parent(Y,Z).
```

We might also make changes to the facts. So mutated versions of the knowledge base could have rules removed:

```
parent(ann,bob).
parent(alec,bob).
parent(alec,billy).
    .
    .
```

rules added:

```
parent(ann,bob).
parent(alec,bob).
parent(ann,billy).
parent(alec,billy).
parent(sarah,billy).
    .
    .
```

or rules changed:

```
parent(ann,bob).
parent(alec,ann).
parent(ann,billy).
parent(alec,billy).
    .
    .
```

For further reading and discussions on the subject of testing knowledge-based systems see Gupta (1991), Ayel and Laurent (1991), and Kiper (1992), for example.

4.6 CONCLUSION

This chapter has discussed the application of traditional testing techniques to a wide variety of subjects. From dealing with requirements documents we have generated acceptance tests; analysis documents have led to the production of system tests; and from design documents we have generated integration tests. A variety of specification and implementation techniques have been described and the testing of them discussed. Sometimes it has not been possible to come up with prescriptive solutions for the testing of different artefacts—but this has not been the intention. The aim has been to alert the tester to the variety of problems and to suggest solutions where possible. Mostly it has been to show how a vast body of knowledge that has hitherto only been applied to a small class of programs may be used on a wide range of different software products.

5

A CASE STUDY

The purpose of this case study is to show more concrete examples of the application of some of the techniques described in the previous chapter. In addition it will show how test plans can be constructed as we progress through the systems life-cycle. We will see how the early stages of systems development tend to generate 'high-level' test cases which capture the major functionality of the system. As we progress through the life-cycle and have to add more detail into the documentation in the form of design information, module specifications etc., so the test cases become correspondingly more detailed. This use of abstraction within test cases allows us to concentrate on the object under test and hopefully find faults at the level at which we are testing—that is, tests derived from the design should find faults in the design, for example. The case study is necessarily small-scale, otherwise the principles and details of the testing techniques would become lost in solving the problem itself.

5.1 THE CASE STUDY

Dylan Dilly-Dally, a postgraduate student, has for several years maintained a card index file of all the references he has used in researching for his PhD. Despite being a computer science graduate, he has only recently come to think that perhaps his manual bibliography system is not the best way of storing this information, and perhaps developing a system to support it might increase his productivity as a researcher and bring him even closer to that elusive higher degree.

He begins by considering the use to which he puts his existing physical card index system. Dylan only stores two types of reference—books and articles—firmly believing that all other forms of research output (conference papers, internal reports, etc.) will eventually find their way into one of these two forms. He realizes that the 'functions' he performs on his manual bibliography system are limited, but frequent. References are added into the system (how else would he have ended up with eight boxes containing a total of 2735 references?), and occasionally removed and discarded as they fall out of favour with the ever-changing theme of his research. The information on the cards sometimes needs to be corrected or updated and, finally, he is forever searching through the bibliography looking for work by a particular author or on a particular subject. So he decides that the automated system should offer four major functions: add, remove, edit and search.

5.2 ANALYSIS OF REQUIREMENTS

The first stage in the development of the system is the analysis of requirements. This casts the informal description in the previous section into a form that is more suitable for further development (and for the production of test cases). Since this is the first 'formal' document that represents a baseline for development, it also represents the criteria against which the success or failure of the final system should be judged. The tests generated from the requirements represent part of this criteria and thereby constitute our acceptance tests. To assist in their production and analysis, requirements are frequently numbered. The very brief set of requirements for our bibliography system is as follows:

1. A reference may be added into the bibliography providing that it does not already exist.
2. A reference may be removed from the bibliography providing that it does already exist.
3. A reference may be edited and any information pertaining to that reference may be changed.
4. A reference may be searched for, given one of the following criteria:

   (a) One or more author (last) names.
   (b) One or more words present in a title.

   All references matching the criteria are returned.

5.2.1 Testing requirements

One of the simplest tests we can use to derive data from requirements is to perform a 'statement' test. This means going through each one of the requirements in turn and generating appropriate test data. We do not try to combine the test data in any interesting way or examine tempting boundaries. We are merely interested in whether a particular requirement has been implemented. This gives us our first set of acceptance tests which examines the 'top-level' functionality offered by the system. The set of requirements for our case study would encourage us to generate the corresponding set of tests:

1. Add a reference that does not exist and one that does exist.
2. Remove a reference that exists, and one that does not exist.
3. Edit a reference.
4. Search for a reference using:

    (a) One author name and two author names.
    (b) One title word and two title words.

The format of these tests, and corresponding output, is presented in Table 5.1. We could, if we wished, generate some of the actual test data (we do not yet have the details of the format of the reference), but there is no particular advantage to be gained in doing so.

Table 5.1 Acceptance tests based on a 'statement' test of requirements

Acceptance tests – 1	
Input	Expected output
Add a new reference	Reference added to bibliography
Add an existing reference	No change to bibliography
Remove an existing reference	Reference removed from bibliography
Remove a non-existent reference	No change to bibliography
Edit a reference	Bibliography updated with edits
Search for a reference using:	
One author name	Bibliography details returned
Two author names	Bibliography details returned
One title word	Bibliography details returned
Two title words	Bibliography details returned

Having considered statement testing, we now want to examine the potentially more demanding techniques of equivalence partitioning and boundary-value analysis. There are no obvious equivalence partitions for

Equivalence class 1	Equivalence class 2
Word	*Word1 . . . Wordn*

the *add, remove* and *edit* functions. For example, there is nothing to suggest (yet!) that books or papers are handled differently, or that they are categorized according to names or titles. The *search* function does, however, lend itself to examination in this fashion. Both the author name(s) and the title may be composed of one or many words and these represent two equivalence classes. Both these have the same format and are shown above with *word* representing either an author name or a word in the title.

Applying the principles of equivalence partitioning forces us to draw test cases from both of these classes, that is, searching for a one-word author or title using just one word, and searching for a many-worded author or title using one (arbitrary) word (on the basis that any of the words is equally justified and likely to yield the same result).

Examining the second equivalence class further using boundary-value analysis tempts us to select the first word and the last word as search keys and also to select all words as the search key.

We can also use these techniques to generate 'illegal' test data, that is, data that fall outside the bounds of the classes. We could generate data that are unlikely ever to appear within the bibliography database, such as names consisting of numbers and punctuation characters (although limited amounts of punctuation are to be expected). Tempting though this sort of test may be, we should try to concentrate on the higher level functionality of the system. One such test would be to look for an n-worded author or title with $n+1$ words. For example, if in the bibliography there was a work by 'Smith and Jones', then we would not expect this to be retrieved by a search for 'Smith, Jones and Davies' or any other similar permutation. The same applies for titles. Another obvious test is to select data that fall outside the equivalence classes, that is, data that do not appear on the bibliography. We could take this even further and try to search for such things as the first and last references in the database, but at the moment we have no notion of how this is to be implemented, so tests such as this are inappropriate.

At this stage we are still producing test requirements—or test plans— which will be used to produce the actual test data. However, the test requirements we produce will be precise and the actual job of generating the data to fulfil these will be trivial. The full set of test requirements for equivalence partitioning and boundary-value analysis is to be found in Table 5.2. These will be used to augment our set of acceptance tests and so they are labelled 'Acceptance tests – 2'. Note that there are some similarities with the first set of acceptance tests. These will all finally be amalgamated into one set of acceptance tests.

Table 5.2 Acceptance tests based on a equivalence partitioning and boundary value analysis test of requirements

Acceptance tests – 2	
Input	**Expected output**
Search for a single authored reference using:	
One author name	Bibliography details returned
Two author names	Nothing returned
Search for a single word titled reference using:	
One word	Bibliography details returned
Two words	Nothing returned
Search for an n authored reference using:	
One author name	Bibliography details returned
First author name	Bibliography details returned
Last author name	Bibliography details returned
n author names	Bibliography details returned
$n + 1$ author names	Nothing returned
Search for an n word titled reference using:	
One word	Bibliography details returned
First word	Bibliography details returned
Last word	Bibliography details returned
n words	Bibliography details returned
$n + 1$ words	Nothing returned
Search for an non-existent reference using:	
One author name	Nothing returned
Many author names	Nothing returned
One title word	Nothing returned
Many title words	Nothing returned

Cause–effect graphing tends to be useful at the requirements stage since the high level of abstraction and partitioning of the problem often reduces the complexity of the resulting graph. This example is an exception, however, for the opposite reason—it has very little in the way of combinations of inputs (which is when cause–effect graphing tends to generate interesting test cases). For this reason we will not apply cause–effect graphing.

5.3 DATA FLOW DIAGRAMS

Moving on to the next 'stage' of development results in our conducting further analysis on our problem and casting this analysis in different forms—data flow diagrams (DFDs) being one of them. This change in representation, along with the embellished details, means we are able to generate tests that examine in detail each main function offered by the system and the interaction between these functions. These tests will constitute our system-level tests. The four main functions of add, edit, search and remove are captured at the top level of the DFD that is given in Fig. 5.1.

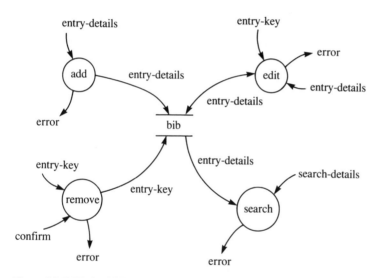

Figure 5.1 DFD for bibliography system.

5.3.1 Data flow testing

Applying data flow testing to DFDs gives us the opportunity to examine the ways in which data are defined and used throughout the system. In our diagram we can see that entry-details occurs frequently at the top level and is therefore a good candidate to examine using this technique (flows that occur infrequently in a diagram—once or twice, say—are not usefully tested using data flow testing).

We can see that entry-details is:

- *Defined* externally to add
- *Used* in add, search and edit
- *Redefined* in edit

So the pairs of definitions and references that we need to look at are:

- add (external) – add
- add (external) – search
- add (external) – edit
- edit – edit
- edit – search
- edit – add ✕

The last one of these represents an infeasible path (or definition-use combination) since we are not able to edit something and then add it to the bibliography—it must already exist. We are then left with five pairs which we need to test. The testing we are encouraged to do is interesting because it forces us to add something to the bibliography to see if we can find it, see if we can change it, and then to change it and still see if it can be found. The set of test data requirements and corresponding output for these data flow tests are shown in Table 5.3.

Table 5.3 System tests based on data flow testing the DFD

System tests – 1	
Input	Expected output
Add a new reference	Reference added to bibliography
Search for newly added reference	Reference found
Edit newly added reference	Bibliography updated with edits
Edit newly edited reference	Bibliography updated with edits
Search for newly edited reference	Reference found

5.3.2 A purely structural approach

Remember that the structural test of a DFD process (or 'bubble') looks to use all inputs and generate all outputs. Applying this to an entire DFD can be difficult due to the large number of tests generated—many of which may be infeasible—so the technique is best limited to either one process or a small number of strongly connected processes. Consider the refinement of the top-level add procedure. This, along with the refinements for the other processes, is shown in Fig. 5.2.

For the refinement of the add process we have three sub-processes: read-and-validate, search-for-duplicates and add-to-bib. To structurally test read-and-validate we need one valid bibliography entry and one invalid one (with a missing author name, for example). To test search-for-duplicates the entry details are passed from read-and-validate and are searched for in the bibliography. To generate an input here, the details must already exist

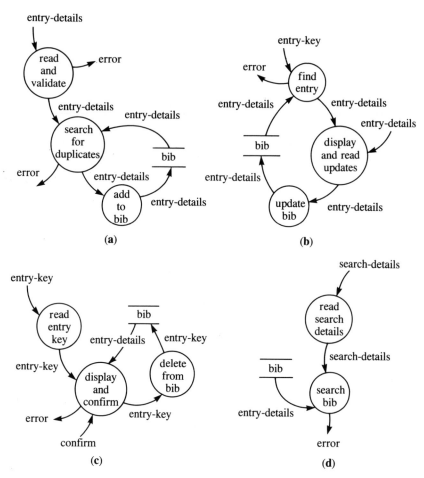

Figure 5.2 Refinements of top-level processes: (a) add process, (b) edit process, (c) remove process, and (d) search process.

in the bibliography and thereby generate an output on the error data flow. To pass on the entry details to add-to-bib, the entry details must not exist on the bibliography and so get added subsequently.

So the structural testing of the refinement of the add process gives us three distinct tests:

- Attempt to add an invalid entry.
- Add an entry that already exists.
- Add an entry that does not exist.

The test requirements for this are formalized in Table 5.4. We could, of course, subject the other process refinements to similar scrutiny.

Table 5.4 System tests based on a structural test of DFD

System tests – 2	
Input	Expected output
Add an invalid reference	Error reported, no change to bibliography
Add an existing reference	Error reported, no change to bibliography
Add a new reference	Reference added to bibliography

5.4 ENTITY–RELATIONSHIP DIAGRAMS

Entity–relationship diagrams (ERDs) provide further analysis information by looking at the relationship between data in the system. This provides a contrast to the purely functional view of the system as afforded by DFDs. This data-oriented view of the system provides a valuable supplement to our existing set of system tests. The ERD for our system is quite straightforward, consisting of a bibliography entity which may have many entries. The entries may be either books or journals. This relationship is shown diagrammatically in Fig. 5.3.

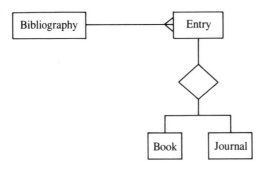

Figure 5.3 Entity–relationship diagram for bibliography system.

Figure 5.3 tells us that there exists a mandatory relationship between bibliography and entry. This means that a bibliography has to have at least one entry—an empty bibliography does not constitute a bibliography. To test this we want to exercise the limits of the relationships between the data by applying our interpretation of boundary-value analysis. In addition, we want to test that the bibliography can hold the two types of data—books and journals. From this we can generate the following 'legal' test cases where k, m and n are arbitrary numbers representing 'many' (or at least two!):

- Bibliography contains one book.
- Bibliography contains one journal.
- Bibliography contains k books.
- Bibliography contains m journals.
- Bibliography contains a mixture of n books and journals.

We can also examine the 'illegal' relationship where a bibliography is empty. That is,

- Bibliography contains zero entries

which, according to our ERD, should not exist.

Merely seeing if the bibliography can 'contain' these entries is not a very demanding test. We also want to see if it can respond to the basic functions applied to this arrangement. So, if we were testing the first of our criteria, we could add one book, search for it, edit it, and finally remove it (which would also test our 'illegal' relationship). Another way to test these relationships would be to set up the bibliography in the ways specified above and apply our set of acceptance tests to these different cases. If we wanted to be even more stringent we could apply the system tests we have developed. The stringency of the testing will depend on such factors as the criticality of the software being developed and the amount of resources available to carry it out. As an example we will show how the first relationship (bibliography contains one book) could be tested with our initial set of acceptance testing criteria (derived from our 'statement-test' of requirements). The test requirements are shown in Table 5.5. Notice that the tests and expected results are basically similar except for the output produced by removing the item from the bibliography. According to our ERD this relationship should not be allowed to hold but there is no mention of what to do anywhere else in the system documentation. Typically we should have to amend the documentation to report an error if this arises, or amend the ERD to somehow make this relationship permissible.

Notice that to be able to carry out the tests detailed in Table 5.5 we would have to ensure that when we came to generate the test data the book had at least two authors and at least two words in the title. Failure to do this would make our `search` function tests infeasible. The other ERD relationships identified could be tested similarly. When the bibliography contained a mixture of books and journals we could either vary the target of our functions (search for a book using one author name and a journal using two, for example) or duplicate the functions for each entry type. Once again it is a question of resources.

Table 5.5 Subset of system tests based on a test of the ERD

System tests – 3	
Input	Expected output
Add one book	Book added to bibliography
Add the existing Book	No change to bibliography
Remove a non-existent reference	No change to bibliography
Edit the book	Bibliography updated with edits
Search for the book using:	
One author name	Bibliography details returned
Two author names	Bibliography details returned
One title word	Bibliography details returned
Two title words	Bibliography details returned
Remove the book	Book removed from bibliography

5.5 ENTITY–LIFE HISTORIES

Our final set of source material for our system tests comes from the entity–life histories (ELHs). Remember that these show the passage of an entity through a system, from its initial conception, or introduction to the system, through all the functions being performed on it, to its eventual demise and disappearance from the system. In using the entity to generate test data we want to examine all its possible states within the system. This gives us a different, and more dynamic, view of the entity than that provided by the ERD. Consider the entity entry in our bibliography system. The possible things that can happen to entry are that it is:

- Added to the bibliography.
- Searched for.
- Edited.
- Removed from the bibliography.

The first of these—adding it to the bibliography—represents the entity's 'birth' in the system, and the final one—removal—represents its 'death'. The other two functions—searching and editing—represent the actions it suffers while 'alive' in the system. The diagrammatic representation of this ELH is shown in Fig. 5.4. Note that we have had to include two 'boxes' above search and edit to show that the entity is stored in the bibliography and referenced many times. Attached to Fig. 5.4 are numbers that represent functions executed at particular stages in the life history. These correspond to the major activities carried out at each stage and are at a fairly high level

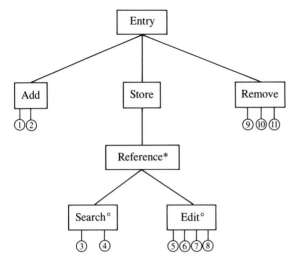

Figure 5.4 Entity–life history for entry.

of abstraction (equivalent, say, to the functions that might be identified at the top levels of a DFD). The functions are:

1. Read and validate entry details.
2. Add entry to bibliography.
3. Read search details.
4. Display corresponding entry details.
5. Read entry key.
6. Display for editing.
7. Read updated detail.
8. Write updated entry to bibliography.
9. Read entry key.
10. Display for confirmation.
11. Remove from bibliography.

Note that we are considering an entity in the system, and writing the functions from the entity's point of view in terms of the actions suffered by it. This means that we do not have to consider adding invalid data (it does not constitute an entity) or being unable to find an entity (the entity would be unaware of this).

In deriving tests from the ELH we want to look at the possible life histories experienced by the entity. These are controlled by the selections and iterations within our diagram. We want to execute the iterative component zero, once and many times. We will perform the single iteration twice—once with the search function, the second time with the edit function—to avoid any possible bias. When iterating many times we will choose the arbitrary number 4, to allow two searches and two edits. This gives us the following possible entity–life histories for `entry`:

- Add, Store, Remove (zero iterations)
- Add, Search, Remove
- Add, Edit, Remove
- Add, Search, Edit, Search, Edit, Remove

This gives us the test requirements shown in Table 5.6 where the double horizontal lines separate distinct sets of test data. We are not constrained to putting just one entry into the bibliography so we do not have to worry about the expected result of removing the entry. What is important is that all the functions manipulate the *same* entry in the bibliography. It is the passage of one entry through the system that we wish to test, not the general behaviour of all entries.

Table 5.6 Subset of system tests based on a test of the ERD

System tests – 4	
Input	Expected output
Add a book Remove the book	Book added to bibliography Book removed from bibliography
Add a book Search for the book Remove the book	Book added to bibliography Bibliography details returned Book removed from bibliography
Add a book Edit the book Remove the book	Book added to bibliography Bibliography updated with edits Book removed from bibliography
Add a book Search for the book Edit the book Search for the book Edit the book Remove the book	Book added to bibliography Bibliography details returned Bibliography updated with edits Bibliography details returned Bibliography updated with edits Book removed from bibliography

5.6 DESIGNS

The design stages represent the casting of the system into some form of structure that details the communication between components. This provides us with excellent information upon which to build our integration tests. The design for the bibliography system is shown in Fig. 5.5. As may be seen, the system consists of four distinct components, representing the major functions of the system, with little interaction between these components. The final implementation would probably see this being built as a menu-driven system.

When generating integration test data we first want to test individual modules and then gradually incorporate the modules together. Our system does not pass many parameters around so we cannot exercise the idea of gradually increasing the number of parameters passed as described in the previous chapter. Another decision to make is whether to integrate the modules top-down or bottom-up. As an example we will show how the `remove` function may be integration tested in a bottom-up fashion. We assume that the modules have been individually tested and we now want to examine their behaviour when called from another module. The low-level functions are `read-key` (which just prompts for and returns an entry key), `display-and-confirm` (which displays the details and prompts for confirmation that the entry is to be deleted), and `delete-from-bib` (which deletes the entry from the bibliography). We would start off by calling these individually from the `remove` function and observing their results. Having done this we can then exercise how the functions pass on data to other functions and we can use the data flow definitions and usages to direct this. Notice that `entry-key` is initially defined in `read-key` and then passed on to `display-and-confirm`, where it is used to retrieve the bibliography entry. This linking together of two modules represents our next integration test. Finally, we examine the entire passage of `entry-key` from its definition in `read-key`, through its usage in `display-and-confirm` to its final usage in `delete-from-bib`. Once this has been done, all three modules are linked together by the `remove` function. The other three functions would be integrated in a similar fashion.

Our integration test requirements are shown in Table 5.7 (on page 137). The double horizontal lines demarcate distinct sets of test data.

5.7 SPECIFICATIONS

The final product of the software design process, prior to implementation, is a set of specifications. The amount of detail, level of abstraction and form of representation is highly dependent on the organization developing the software. Specifications describe in detail the functions performed by, for example, one process in a DFD or one module in a design. They are used to provide the 'black-box' tests for the corresponding unit or module.

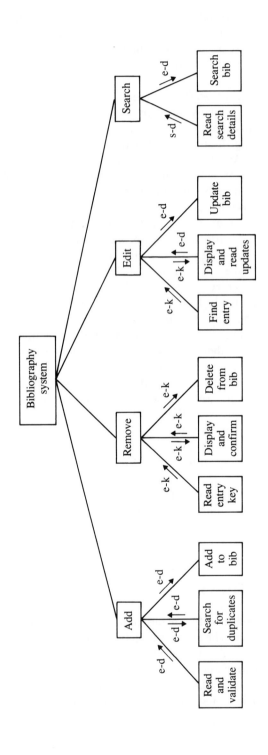

Key:

e-d = entry-details
e-k = entry-key
s-d = search-details

Figure 5.5 Design for bibliography system.

Table 5.7 Subset of integration tests based on design information

Integration tests	
Input	Expected output
Entry key	Entry key
Entry key	Bibliography details returned
Entry key	Book removed from bibliography
Entry key	Bibliography details returned
Entry key	Book removed from bibliography

5.7.1 Natural language

Consider the specification for the simple process, `read-search-details`. In our requirements we noted that:

- A reference may be searched for given one of the following criteria:

  1. One or more author (last) names.
  2. One or more words present in a title.

A natural language specification for this might typically contain the following information:

- `read-search-details`: The user is prompted for the type of search details—either author names or title words. They are then required to enter at least one name, or word, corresponding to their choice. This list of names or words is returned.

   Looking at the specification above we need to consider two inputs. The first defines the type of search details, and equivalence partitioning (or common sense!) would prompt us to test the possibilities or 'author', 'title' and something invalid ('journal name' for example). The second input is the names, or words, to be searched for. We are required to input at least one name and there is no suggestion in the specification that the number of names, or words, in any way affects the processing. This gives us an equivalence class of one to many names (or words). Applying boundary value analysis would obviously tempt us to try one name (or word). We also need to choose an arbitrary number falling somewhere in the equivalence class—say three—and input this number of names and words. Finally, we want to test the response to inputting zero names or words. The test requirements for the read-search-details are shown in Table 5.8.

The lack of combinations of inputs prevents cause–effect graphing or category–partition testing from being of much use in this case.

Table 5.8 Unit tests based on read-search-details **specification**

Unit tests – 1	
Input	Expected output
Search for author name	Prompt for author name
One author name	One author name
Three author names	Three author names
No author names	Error
Search for title word	Prompt for title word
One title word	One title word
Three title words	Three title words
No title words	Error
Search for journal name	Error

5.7.2 Structured English

A more formal representation of a specification is Structured English. This pseudo-code type of language removes some of the ambiguities of natural language by making the scope of decisions and conditions more visible. It also has the advantage of being in a form that lets us apply many of the structural testing techniques to generate test data. Consider again the search function performed by the system, but this time we will look at the search-bib process. Referring again to our requirements we have:

- A reference may be searched for given one of the following criteria:

  1. One or more author (last) names.
  2. One or more words present in a title.

  All references matching the criteria are returned.

The only clue we have as to what this process should do is the last sentence,

All references matching the criteria are returned.

A Structured English specification for this process is given below:

```
read search-type {author or title - passed as parameter}
read search-details {author or title words - passed as parameter}
repeat
   read bib-entry
   if bib-entry = book then
      if search-details = author then
         if bib-entry.book.author-name contains search-details
            display bib-entry
         endif
      else
         if bib-entry.book.title contains search-details
            display bib-entry
         endif
      endif
   else {its a journal}
      if search-details = author then
         if bib-entry.journal.author-name contains search-details
            display bib-entry
         endif
      else
         if bib-entry.journal.title contains search-details
            display bib-entry
         endif
      endif
   endif
until bib-entry = null {end of bibliography}
```

Applying branch coverage to this example requires us to exercise the true and false outcomes of each condition. Consider, first of all, searching for a book. This means placing at least two items in the bibliography, searching the bibliography using an author name and finding one matching entry, then searching the bibliography using the title words and finding one matching entry. This has to be repeated for journals. This gives us the test requirements shown in Table 5.9.

Another way of testing the specification above is to apply the data flow testing technique. If we looked at the bib-entry 'variable' which is defined at the beginning of the repeat-loop, referenced each time it is displayed when a matching entry is found and in the until-condition, this would force us to come up with one extra test corresponding to the initial definition and this last reference in the until-condition. To test this we would want nothing returned from the search—that is, no entries matching the search details. We shall not generate a table for this set of tests. If we

Table 5.9 Unit tests based on `search-bib` specification

Unit tests – 2	
Input	Expected output
Add book1	Book1 added to bibliography
Add book2	Book2 added to bibliography
Add journal1	Journal1 added to bibliography
Add journal2	Journal2 added to bibliography
Search for book1 using author name	Bibliography details returned for book1
Search for book1 using title	Bibliography details returned for book1
Search for journal1 using author name	Bibliography details returned for journal1
Search for journal1 using title	Bibliography details returned for journal1

wished, we could augment the branch coverage tests. As the reader should be aware, we can apply other structural techniques with similar ease.

5.8 CONCLUSION

This small case study has demonstrated how we can use a variety of software products—specifications, designs, etc.—to generate test data requirements for the corresponding life-cycle stage. All that remains to be done is to substitute actual test data for these requirements, once we know the required format for the input data. Obviously we have not finished generating our test requirements. While we were able to generate fairly comprehensive sets of tests for the early stages, we have had to be selective when dealing with some of the analysis documents, designs, and specifications. We have also observed how the test data requirements have become more detailed as we progress through the life-cycle stages. That is, tests have been generated at the appropriate level of abstraction. Our final set of tests would, of course, come from the programs themselves—and the reader has at his or her disposal a variety of techniques to apply at this stage.

BIBLIOGRAPHY

Adrion, W. R., Branstad, M. A. and Cherniavsky, J. C. (1982) 'Validation, Verification and Testing of Computer Software', *ACM Computing Surveys*, **14** (2), June, 159–192.

Ayel, M. and Laurent, J-P. (1991) *Validation, Verification and Tests of Knowledge. Based Systems*, Wiley.

Basili, V. R. and Perricone, B. T. (1984) 'Software Errors and Complexity: An Empirical Investigation', *CACM*, **27** (1), January, 42–52.

Basili, V. R. and Selby, R. W. (1987) 'Comparing the Effectiveness of Software Testing Strategies', *IEEE Transactions on Software Engineering*, **SE-13** (12), December, 1278–1296.

Beizer, B. (1983) *Software Testing Techniques*, Van Nostrand Reinhold.

Bieman, J. M. and Schultz, J. L. (1989) 'Estimating the Number of Test Cases Required to Satisfy the All-du-Paths Testing Criterion'. In R. A. Kemmerer (ed.), *Proceedings of the ACM SIGSOFT 89 3rd Symposium on Software Testing, Analysis and Verification (TAV3)*, ACM, December, 179–186.

Boehm, B. W. (1978) 'The High Cost of Software'. In E. Miller and W. E. Howden (eds), *Tutorial: Software Testing and Validation Techniques*, IEEE, pp. 377–388.

Bougé, L., Choquet, N., Fribourg, L and Gaudel, M-C. (1986) 'Test Sets Generation from Algebraic Specifications using Logic Programming', *Journal of Systems and Software*, **6** (4), November, 343–360.

Bowen, J. B. (1980) 'Standard Errors Classification to Support Software Reliability Assessment'. In *National Computing Conference Proceedings*, Vol. 49, pp. 697–705.

Brinch Hansen, P. (1978) 'Reproducible Testing of Monitors', *Software—Practice and Experience*, **8**, 721–729.

Brown, J. R. (1972) *Practical Application of Automated Software Tools*. Technical Report TRW-SS-72-05, TRW.

Budd, T. A. (1983) 'Techniques for Advanced Software Validation'. In *Infotech State of the Art Report 11:3, Software Engineering: Developments*, Pergamon Infotech International Ltd, ch. 2, pp. 17–36.

Cherniavsky, J. C. and Statman, R. (1988) 'Testing: An Abstract Approach'. In *Proceedings of the 2nd Workshop on Software Testing, Verification and Analysis*, IEEE, pp. 38–44.

Choquet, N. (1986) 'Test Data Generation Using a Prolog with Constraints'. In *Proceedings of the Workshop on Software Testing*. IEEE.

Chusho, T. (1983) 'Coverage Measure for Path Testing Based on the Concept of Essential Branches', *Journal of Information Processing (JAPAN)*, **6** (4), 199–205.

Clarke, L. A. (1979) 'Automatic Test Data Selection Techniques'. In *Infotech State of the Art Report—Software Testing*, Infotech International Ltd.

Clarke, L. A., Hassell, J. and Richardson, D. J. (1982) 'A Close Look at Domain Testing', *IEEE Transactions on Software Engineering*, **SE-8** (4), July, 380–390.

Clarke, L. A., Podgurski, A., Richardson, D. J. and Zeil, S. J. (1985) 'A comparison of data flow path selection criteria'. In *Proceedings of the 8th International Conference on Software Engineering*, IEEE, August, pp. 244–251.

Clarke, L. A. and Richardson, D. J. (1983a) 'The Application of Error-sensitive Testing Strategies to Debugging'. In *Proceedings of the ACM SIGSOFT/SIGPLAN Software Engineering Symposium on High-Level Debugging*, pp. 45–52.

Clarke, L. A. and Richardson, D. J. (1983b) 'A Rigorous Approach to Error-sensitive Testing'. In *Proceedings of the 16th Annual Hawaii International Conference on System Sciences*, pp. 197–206.

Dahl, O.-J., Dijkstra, E. W. and Hoare, C. A. R. (1972) *Structured Programming*, Academic Press.

DeMillo, R. A., Guindi, D. S., McCracken, W. M., Offutt, A. J. and King, K. N. (1988) 'An Extended Overview of the Mothra Software Testing Environment'. In *Proceedings of the 2nd Workshop on Software Testing, Verification, and Analysis*, IEEE, pp. 142–151.

DeMillo, R. A., Lipton, R. J. and Sayward, F. J. (1978) 'Hints on Test Data Selection: Help for the Practising Programmer', *Computer*, **11** (4), April, 34–41.

DeMillo, R. A., McCracken, W. M., Martin, R. J. and Passafiume, J. F. (1987) *Software Testing and Evaluation*, Benjamin Cummings.

DeMillo, R. A. and Offutt, A. J. (1991) 'Constraint-based Automatic Test Data Generation', *IEEE Transactions on Software Engineering*, **17** (9), September, 900–910.

Deutsch, M. S. (1982) *Software Verification and Validation—Realistic Project Approaches*, Prentice-Hall.

Duncan, A. G. (1978) 'Test Grammars: A Method for Generating Program Test Data'. In *Digest for the Workshop on Software Testing and Test Documentation*, pp. 270–283.

Elmendorf, W. R. (1973) *Cause Effect Graphs in Functional Testing*. Technical Report TR.00.2487, IBM Dev. Dev. Poughkeepsie.

Endres, A. (1975) 'An Analysis of Errors and their Causes in System Programs'. In *Proceedings of the International Conference on Reliable Software*, IEEE.

Forman, I. (1984) 'An Algebra for Data Flow Anomaly Detection'. In *Proceedings of the IEEE 7th International Conference on Software Engineering*, IEEE, March, pp. 278–286.

Gannon, J. D., McMullin, P. and Hamlet, R. (1981) 'Data Abstraction, Implementation, Specification and Testing', *ACM TOPLAS*, **3** (3), July.

Girgis, M. R. and Woodward, M. R. (1985) 'An Integrated System for Program Testing using Weak Mutation and Data Flow Analysis'. In *Proceedings of the 8th International Conference on Software Engineering*, IEEE, August, pp. 313–319.

Girgis, M. R. and Woodward, M. R. (1986) 'An Experimental Comparison of the Error Exposing Ability of Program Testing Criteria'. In *Proceedings of the Workshop on Software Testing*, IEEE, July, pp. 64–73.

Glass, R. L. (1979) *Software Reliability Guidebook*, Prentice-Hall.

Glass, R. L. (1981) 'Persistent Software Errors', *IEEE Transactions on Software Engineering*, **7** (2), March, 162–168.

Goodenough, J. B. and Gerhart, S. L. (1975) 'Toward a Theory of Test Data Selection'. *IEEE Transactions on Software Engineering*, SE-1(2), June, 156–173.

Gourlay, J. S. (1984) 'Introduction to the Formal Treatment of Testing'. In H-L. Hausen (ed.), *Software Validation*, North-Holland, pp. 67–72.

Gupta, U. (ed.) (1991) *Validating and Verifying Knowledge-Based Systems*. IEEE Computer Society Press.

Haley, A. and Zweben, S. (1984) 'Development and Application of a White Box Approach to Integration Testing', *The Journal of Systems and Software*, **4**, 309–315.

Hall, P. A. V. and Hierons, R. (1991) *Formal Methods and Testing*, Technical Report 91/16, Computing Dept, The Open University.

Hamlet, R. and Taylor, R. (1990) 'Partition Testing Does Not Inspire Confidence', *IEEE Transactions on Software Engineering*, **16** (12), December, 1402–1411.

Harrold, M. J., McGregor, J. D. and Fitzpatrick, K. J. (1992) 'Incremental Testing of Object-oriented Structures'. In *Proceedings of the International Conference on Software Engineering*, IEEE, pp. 68–80.

Harrold, M J. and Soffa, M. J. (1991) 'Selecting and Using Data for Integration Testing', *IEEE Software*, **8** (2), March, 58–65.

Hedley, D. and Hennell, M. A. (1985) 'The Causes and Effects of Infeasible Paths in Computer Programs'. In *Proceedings of the 8th International Conference on Software Engineering*, IEEE, August, pp. 259–266.

Henderson, P. (1985) 'Specifications and Programs'. In T. A. Anderson (ed.), *Software—Requirements, Specification and Testing*, Blackwell Scientific Publications, ch. 8, pp. 75–82.

Hennell, M. A., Hedley, D. and Riddell, I. J. (1983) 'The LDRA Software Testbeds: Their Roles and Capabilities'. In *IEEE Software '83 Conference*, IEEE, pp. 69–77.

Hennell, M. A., Hedley, D. and Riddell, I. J. (1984) 'Assessing a Class of Software Tools'. In *Proceedings of the IEEE 7th International Conference on Software Engineering*, IEEE, March, pp. 266–277.

Hetzel, W. C. (1976) *An Experimental Analysis of Program Verification Methods*, PhD thesis, University of North Carolina.

Hetzel, W. C. (1985) *The Complete Guide to Software Testing*, Collins.

Hoffman, D. M. and Strooper, P. (1991) 'Automated Module Testing in Prolog', *IEEE Transactions on Software Engineering*, **17** (9), September, 934–943.

Hoffman, R. H. (1975) 'NASA/Johnson Space Center Approach to Automated Test Data Generation'. In *Proceedings of the Computer Science and Statistics 8th Annual Symposium on the Interface*, NASA.

Houghton, R. C. Jr. (1982) *Software Development Tools*. Technical Report NBS Special Publication 500-88, National Bureau of Standards.

Howden, W. E. (1976) 'Reliability of the Path Analysis Testing Strategy', *IEEE Transactions on Software Engineering*, SE-2 (3), September, 208–215.

Howden, W. E. (1978) 'Theoretical and Empirical Studies of Program Testing', *IEEE Transactions on Software Engineering*, **SE-4** (4), July, 293–298.

Howden, W. E. (1981) 'Completeness Criteria for Testing Elementary Program Functions'. In *Proceedings of the 5th International Conference on Software Engineering*, IEEE, March, pp. 235–243.

Howden, W. E. (1982a) 'Validation of Scientific Programs', *ACM Computing Surveys*, **14** (2), June, 193–227.

Howden, W. E. (1982b) 'Weak Mutation Testing and Completeness of Test Sets', *IEEE Transactions on Software Engineering*, **SE-8** (4), July, 371–379.

Huang, J. C. (1975) 'An Approach to Program Testing', *Computing Surveys*, **7** (3), September, 113–127.

Ihm, H.-S. and Ntafos, S. C. (1983) 'Rets: Required Element Testing Systems'. In *Proceedings of the Symposium Application and Assessment of Automated Tools for Software Development*.

Ince, D. (1988) *Fashioning the Baroque*, Oxford Science Publications.

Ince, D. (1991) *Object-Oriented Software Engineering with C++*, McGraw-Hill.

Jachner, J. and Agarwal, V. K. (1984) 'Data Flow Anomaly Detection', *IEEE Transactions on Software Engineering*, **SE-10** (4), July, 432–437.

Jackson, M. A. (1975) *Principles of Program Design*, Academic Press.

Jones, C. B. (1986) *Systematic Software Development Using VDM*, Prentice-Hall.

Kiper, J. D. (1992) 'Structural Testing of Rule-Based Expert Systems', *ACM Transactions on Software Engineering and Methodology*, **1** (2), April, 168–187.

Korel, B. (1990) 'Automated Software Test Data Generation', *IEEE Transactions on Software Engineering*, **16** (8), August, 870–879.

Kundu, S. (1979) 'Setar—New Approach to Test Case Generation'. In *Infotech State of the Art Report—Software Testing*, Infotech International Ltd.

Laski, J. W. and Korel, B. (1983) 'A Data Flow Oriented Program Testing Strategy', *IEEE Transactions on Software Engineering*, **SE-9** (3), May, 347–354.

Lauterbach, L. and Randall, W. (1989) 'Experimental Evaluation of Six Test Techniques'. In *Proceedings of Compass 89*, ACM Press, pp. 36–41.

Lesniak-Betley, A. M. (1984) 'Audit of Statement Analysis Methodology'. In *Proceedings of the 3rd Annual International Phoenix Conference on Computers and Communications*, March, pp. 174–180.

Lientz, B. P. and Swanson, E. B. (1980) *Software Maintenance Management*, Addison-Wesley.

Lipow, M. (1975) 'Some Directed Graph Methods for Analyzing Computer Programs'. In *Proceedings of Computer Science and Statistics 8th Annual Symposium on the Interface*, pp. 357–363.

Lutz, M. (1990) 'Testing Tools', *IEEE Software*, **7** (3), May, 53–57.

Marimont, R. B. (1960) 'Applications of Graphs and Boolean Matrices to Computer Programming', *SIAM Review*, **2** (4), October, 259–268.

Maurer, P. M. (1990) 'Generating Test Data with Enhanced Context-free Grammars'. *IEEE Software*, **7** (4), July, 50–55.

McCabe, T. J. (1976) 'A Complexity Measure', *IEEE Transactions on Software Engineering*, **SE-2** (4), December, 308–320.

McCabe, T. J. and Schulmeyer, G. G. (1985) 'System Testing Aided by Structured Analysis: A Practical Experience', *IEEE Transactions on Software Engineering*, **SE-11** (9), September, 917–921.

Myers, G. J. (1976) *Software Reliability—Principles and Practices*, Wiley.

Myers, G. J. (1979) *The Art of Software Testing*, Wiley.

NCC (1989) *Software Tools for Verification, Validation and Testing*. NCC Publications.

Ntafos, S. C. (1984) 'On Required Element Testing', *IEEE Transactions on Software Engineering*, **SE-10** (6), November, 795–803.

Ntafos, S. C. (1988) A Comparison of Some Structural Testing Strategies', *IEEE Transactions on Software Engineering*, **14** (6), June, 868–874.

Offutt, A. J. (1989) 'The Coupling Effect: Fact or Fiction'. In R. A. Kemmerer (ed.), *Proceedings of ACM SIGSOFT 89 3rd Symposium on Software Testing, Analysis and Verification (TAV3)*, ACM Press, pp. 131–140.

O'Keefe, R., Balci, O. and Smith, E. (1991) 'Validating Expert System Performance'. In Uma Gupta (ed.), *Validating and Verifying Knowledge-Based Systems*, IEEE Computer Society Press.

Osterweil, L. J. (1977) 'The Detection of Unexecutable Program Paths through Static Data Flow Analysis'. In *Proceedings of COMPSAC 77*, IEEE, November, pp. 406–413.

Ostrand, T. J. and Balcer, M. J. (1988) 'The Category–Partition Method for Specifying and Generating Functional Tests', *Communications of the ACM*, **31** (6), June, 676–686.

Ostrand, T. J. and Weyuker, E. J. (1984) 'Collecting and Categorizing Software Error Data in an Industrial Environment', *The Journal of Systems and Software*, **4** (4), November, 289–300.

Ould, M. A. and Unwin, C. (eds) (1986) *Testing in Software Development*, Cambridge University Press.

Paige, M. R. (1978) 'An Analytical Approach to Software Testing'. In *Proceedings of Compsac '78*, IEEE, November, pp. 527–532.

Paige, M. R. and Holthouse, M. A. (1977) 'On Sizing Software Testing for Structured Programs'. In *International Symposium of Fault Tolerant Computing*, June, p. 212.

Perry, D. E. and Kaiser, G. E. (1990) 'Adequate Testing and Object-oriented Programming', *Journal of Object Oriented Programming*, **2** (5), January/February, 13–19.

Prather, R. E. (1983) 'Theory of Program Testing—An Overview', *The Bell System Technical Journal*, **62** (10(ii)), December.

Prather, R. E. and Myers, J. P. Jr. (1987) 'The Path Prefix Software Testing Strategy', *IEEE Transactions on Software Engineering*, **SE-13** (7), July, 761–765.

Rapps, S. and Weyuker, E. J. (1985) 'Selecting Software Test Data Using Data Flow Information', *IEEE Transactions on Software Engineering*, **SE-11** (4), April, 367–375.

Richardson, D. J. and Clarke, L. A. (1981) 'A Partition Analysis Method to Increase Program Reliability'. In *Proceedings of the 5th International Conference on Software Engineering*, IEEE, March, pp. 244–253.

Richardson, D. J. and Clarke, L. A. (1985a) 'Partition Analysis: A Method Combining Testing and Verification', *IEEE Transactions on Software Engineering*, **SE-11** (12), December, 1477–1490.

Richardson, D. J. and Clarke, L. A. (1985b) 'Testing Techniques Based on Symbolic Evaluation'. In T. Anderson (ed.), *Software—Requirements, Specification and Testing*, Blackwell Scientific Publications pp. 93–110.

Roper, M. and Smith, P. (1987) 'A Structural Testing Method for JSP Designed Programs', *Software—Practice and Experience*, **17** (2), February, 135–157.

Rubey, R. J., Dana, J. A. and Biche, P. W. (1975) 'Quantitative Aspects of Software Validation', *IEEE Transactions on Software Engineering*, **1** (2), June, 150–155.

Schneidewind, N. F. and Hoffman, M. (1979) 'An Experiment on Software Error Data Collection and Analysis', *IEEE Transactions on Software Engineering*, **SE-5** (3), May, 276–286.

Shaw, M. (1990) 'Prospects for an engineering discipline of software', *IEEE Software*, **7** (6), November, 15–24.

Smith, M. D. and Robson, D. J. (1990) 'Object-oriented Programming—the Problems of Validation'. In *Proceedings of the Conference on Software Maintenance 1990*, IEEE Computer Society Press, November, pp. 272–281.

Tai, K. C. (1989) 'Testing of Concurrent Software'. In *Proceedings of the 13th Annual International Computer Software and Applications Conference*, IEEE Computer Society Press, pp. 62–64.

Taylor, R. N., Levine, D. L. and Kelly, C. D. (1992) 'Structural Testing of Concurrent Programs', *IEEE Transactions on Software Engineering*, **18** (3), March, 206–215.

Turski, W. M. and Maibaum, T. S. E. (1987) *The Specification of Computer Programs*, Addison-Wesley.

Werner, L. L. (1986) 'A Study of "Hard to Find" Data Processing Errors'. In *Proceedings of the ACM 14th Annual Computer Science Conference*, p. 410.

Weyuker, E. J. (1979) 'The Applicability of Program Schema Results to Programs', *International Journal of Computer Information Science*, **8**, October, 387–403.

Weyuker, E. J. (1988a) 'The Evaluation of Program-based Software Test Data Adequacy Criteria', *Communications of the ACM*, **31** (6), June, 668–675.

Weyuker, E. J. (1988b) 'An Empirical Study of the Complexity of Data Flow Testing'. In *Proceedings of the 2nd Workshop on Software Testing, Verification and Analysis*, IEEE, July, pp. 188–195.

Weyuker, E. J. and Jeng, B. (1991) 'Analyzing Partition Testing Strategies', *IEEE Transactions on Software Engineering*, **17** (7), July, 703–711.

Weyuker, E. J. and Ostrand, T. J. (1980) 'Theories of Program Testing and the Application of Revealing Subdomains', *IEEE Transactions on Software Engineering*, **SE-6** (3), May, 236–246.

White, L. J. (1985) 'Domain Testing and Several Outstanding Problems in Program Testing', *INFOR*, **23** (1), February, 53–68.

White, L. J. and Cohen, E. I. (1980) 'A Domain Strategy for Computer Program Testing', *IEEE Transactions on Software Engineering*, **SE-6** (3), May, 247–257.

Woodward, M. R. (1984) 'An Investigation into Program Paths and their Representation', *Technology and Science of Informatics*, **3** (4), 221–228.

Woodward, M. R. (1989) *Mutation Testing of Algebraic Specifications*. Technical Report 89/2, Dept of Computer Science, University of Liverpool.

Woodward, M. R. and Halewood, K. (1988) 'From Weak to Strong, Dead or Alive? An Analysis of Some Mutation Testing Issues'. In *Proceedings of the 2nd Workshop on Software Testing, Verification, and Analysis*, IEEE, July, pp. 152–158.

Woodward, M. R., Hedley, D. and Hennell, M. A. (1980) 'Experience with Path Analysis and Testing of Programs', *IEEE Transactions on Software Engineering*, **SE-6** (3), May, 278–286.

Wu, D., Hennell, M. A., Hedley, D. and Riddell, I. J. (1988) 'A Practical Method for Software Quality Control via Program Mutation'. In *Proceedings of the 2nd Workshop on Software Testing, Verification, and Analysis*, IEEE, July, pp. 159–170.

Yang, R. D. and Chung, C.-G. (1990) 'A Path Analysis Approach to Concurrent Program Testing'. In *Proceedings of the 9th Annual Phoenix Conference on Computers and Communications*, pp. 425–432.

INDEX